D1601466

UNDERSTANDING AND WORKING WITH THE JAPANESE BUSINESS WORLD

Hiroki Kato
Joan S. Kato

PRENTICE HALL
Englewood Cliffs, New Jersey 07632

Prentice-Hall International (UK) Limited, *London*
Prentice-Hall of Australia Pty. Limited, *Sydney*
Prentice-Hall Canada, Inc., *Toronto*
Prentice-Hall Hispanoamericana, S.A., *Mexico*
Prentice-Hall of India Private Limited, *New Delhi*
Prentice-Hall of Japan, Inc., *Tokyo*
Simon & Schuster Asia Pte. Ltd., *Singapore*
Editora Prentice-Hall do Brasil, Ltda., *Rio de Janeiro*

© 1992 *by*

PRENTICE-HALL, Inc.

Englewood Cliffs, NJ

10 9 8 7 6 5 4 3 2 1

Library of Congress Cataloging-in-Publication Data

Kato, Hiroki.
Understanding and working with the Japanese business world / by Hiroki and Joan Stern
Kato.
    p.   cm.

  Includes index.
  ISBN 0-13-155839-0
  1. Business communication—Japan. 2. Business communication—United States. I. Kato, Joan
Stern. II. Title.
HF5718.2.J3K38   1992
395'.52'0952—dc20   91-35259
                                                                 CIP

0-13-155839-0

PRENTICE HALL
Business Information & Publishing Division
Englewood Cliffs, NJ 07632
Simon & Schuster, A Paramount Communications Company

PRINTED IN THE UNITED STATES OF AMERICA

Dedicated to Yukie and Michiaki, to Joseph, to the memory of Tania, to Isaac Ken and Saul Sen, and to the other members of our families on both sides of the Pacific.

Preface

It was not until after we made a commitment to our publisher at Prentice Hall, that we realized that our eagerness to write this book grew out of mutual affirmation of many years of trying to understand each other. Of course, when we met as university students, who would have guessed it would have been an issue?

Suspicions were aroused three weeks into the marriage when Hiroki, a person of no mean education, said he "caught a cold through his stomach," something that is simply not done in America. The ensuing two hour discourse on the pathogenesis of infectious disease convinced no one. There was definitely a cultural difference here. It seems that how you catch a cold depends a lot on where you were raised.

In the subsequent 24 years, we have had even stranger conversations, often about whether Western-style conversations have any merit anyway.

Our home life has been sort of a cross-cultural lab. We think we have proven a couple of things, pretty obvious now, that we hadn't even hypothesized when we started: (1) that it is more difficult to communicate with someone from a different culture than with someone who possesses the same points of cultural reference; (2) that despite good intentions and best efforts, in the absence of mutual cultural knowledge, an impasse in communication arises quickly and inevitably; and (3) that cross-cultural communication flourishes in direct proportion to mutual cultural knowledge and experience.

Much of what we have learned in our domestic "lab," augmented by research, we have applied in our professional and business endeavors. We have observed over and over situations in which American and Japanese businesspeople missed opportunities or wasted time because neither side knew what the other wanted or meant. Goodwill and the motivation to do the deal are simply not enough. We are sure that American and Japanese businesspeople need mutual cultural knowledge—both to work together and to compete rationally.

Our mission here is to focus on communication—on understanding what meaning a Japanese businessperson intends, whether he is communicating in English or in Japanese, at home or abroad—and on how a Japanese businessperson will interpret what his American counterpart says, does, or does not say. Although parts of the book offer specific practical advice, no practical guide on how to interpret the meaning of a communication is complete without an understanding of the principals of the culture of the communicator. In other words, no level of mastery of Japanese grammar or knowledge of Japanese vocabulary, unless coupled with a thorough knowledge of Japanese culture, is sufficient to understand what a Japanese businessperson means or what he thinks you mean.

This book is organized in four parts. The principles of culture, the theoretical underpinnings of the practical, are found in Part I. The theoretical evolves into the practical in Part II, which deals with Japanese business organizations, how to initiate contacts with them, and what to expect at first meetings. Part III treats various types of verbal communication. And Part IV deals with equally, if not more, important nonverbal communication. Chapters Three through Five of Part I and Parts II, III, and IV contain summary guidelines at the end of each chapter. At the end of the book are a glossary and a guide to pronouncing the Japanese words used in the book.

All the guidelines offered should be viewed far more flexibly than a list of "do's" and "don'ts." A strictly "do's" and "don'ts" approach fails for three reasons. First, it should not be surprising that all Japanese are not alike. Certain aspects of American behavior may be welcomed by some Japanese, incomprehensible to others, and downright offensive to still others. Second, mind-set and specific behavior often depend upon where an individual is placed and with whom. Third, any resemblance between the American and the Japanese version of a specific norm common to both, such as "the customer is king," may be strictly superficial.

We will have achieved our purpose if our readers are better prepared to "size up" and understand the Japanese businesspeople whom they encounter.

Introduction:
Ishin-Denshin

In the mid-1970s, U. S. ambassador to Japan Mike Mansfield advanced the then somewhat startling opinion that the bi-lateral relationship between Japan and the United States is the most important in the world bar none. The thought was startling because to the extent that most Americans had any concept or consciousness of Japan, it was of Japan as a rightfully vanquished enemy on the other side of the world, still dependent upon the United States in its economy and in its foreign policy. Perhaps because of a lack of shared history, language, or culture between these two countries, the notion that by the last quarter of the twentieth century their destinies would be inextricably intertwined was novel.

Today more than 1,045 Japanese companies operate in the United States generating total sales of $185 billion.

Ambassador Mansfield's view is now widely accepted. In fact, the singular importance of the bi-lateral relationship between Japan and the United States has become a commonplace observation in lectures, seminars, and editorials and in any other forum where the topic is the relationship between these two nations. Today more than 1,045 Japanese companies operate in the United States, generating total sales of $185 billion.

Recent convincing evidence of the unprecedented importance of the bi-lateral relationship is the role that Japan has had in supplying the United States with technology and electronic wizardry for weapons crucial to the Allies in the Persian Gulf War. Defense industry sources in both countries agree that up to 80 percent of the components in some of America's "smart" weapons are produced by some 200 Japanese high-tech firms, including the giants such as Toshiba, Mitsubishi Electric, and Sumitomo Electric. Both Patriot and Tomahawk missiles rely on Japanese made computer chips.

In the face of recent dramatic geopolitical lurches and shifts, other bilateral relationships such as those with China, the Soviet Union, or the nations of Eastern Europe may have captured the attention and imagination of American business. However, hope for significant expansion of trade with these countries is premature. The fundamental weak-nesses in their economies, not to mention persistent political uncertainties, extinguish the possibility that they will be anywhere nearly as important to Americans as is Japan—at least for years, if not decades, to come.

Unfortunately, the importance of the bilateral relationship between Japan and the United States to both countries and the rest of the world does not ensure its success. Japanese and Americans often cannot fathom what the other is saying. Prejudice born of ignorance abounds.

The increase in the numbers of Americans and Japanese who work together does not seem to have improved the situation. Xenophobic voices on both sides of the Pacific find ready audiences. In a commercial for an American automaker, aired in the New York metropolitan area, an announcer projects a dark future: "Imagine a few years from now. It's December and the whole family's going to see the big Christmas tree at Hirohito Center. Go on. Keep buying Japanese cars." On the other side of the Pacific, captains of Japanese industry take time to write "America-bashing" books that rack up enviable sales in Japan.

Although strains in the relationship have been evident for some time, they have become the target of particular focus as the trade imbalance in Japan's favor remains substantially unabated. Japan's economic power rankles many Americans who believe that it was built, in part, at the expense of American industry. They resent that the Japanese manage to buy American landmarks and expensive golf courses and do not believe that the Japanese carry their fair share of the burdens of international citizenship in the form of an adequate defense budget.

On the other hand, it rankles many Japanese that despite their country's economic power, Americans are largely ignorant about Japan. A Japanese history professor was recently quoted as saying,

> In my travels through America I am appalled at how ignorant the average American is about Japan, how superficial the media is in their interest of [sic] the Japanese, how biased Americans are toward Europe. Yet no country in the past 40 years has had such an impact on American industry, the American economy and the American living standard as Japan.[1]

There is some justification for Japanese impatience with Americans' lack of knowledge about Japan. Approximately 25,000 Japanese students study in the United States annually, while only 1,000 American students go to Japan.

Historically, there has been a lag between the growth of Japan's economic power and the amount of readily available information about the Japanese and their culture. Even by the time that the United States had accrued a huge trade deficit with Japan, only a small number of Americans were well acquainted with the country and its people.

This lag may rest on the fact that the United States remains a net exporter of culture to Japan. While the Japanese have not, or are likely to, become socially "Westernized," Japanese devour American music, movies, and the secular aspects of American holidays. Currently, there is even a strong Japanese market for American memorabilia from the 1950s and 1960s. However, the cultural "trade imbalance" in favor of the United States only partially explains Americans' general ignorance about Japan.

Approximately 25,000 Japanese students study in the United States annually, while only 1,000 American students go to Japan.

The situation began to change in the mid-1980s. Today it is difficult to pick up a major American newspaper without reading a story related to Japan. Each morning the closing price of the Nikkei 225 stock index is announced on all three television networks, and prices of the shares of companies listed on the Tokyo Stock Exchange appear in the financial pages of general newspapers. Even American public schools at the elementary and secondary levels are revising their curricula to include information about Japan. Some are even beginning to offer Japanese language courses. At the college level, the number of students who study Japanese has finally increased more than fourfold in the last decade.

---

[1]Professor Etsuji Takikawa, as quoted in Ronald E. Yates, "Japanese Spending $370 Million to Polish Tarnished Image in U.S.," *The Chicago Tribune,* January 6, 1991, p. 16.

However, the problem of communication between Americans and Japanese is complicated because Japanese conceptualize the process of communication so differently from Americans. A typical Japanese view of communication is captured in the expression *ishin-denshin,* which means that "if it is in one heart, it will be transmitted to another heart." That is, what you are thinking can be communicated without using the medium of words if both parties are sincere.

Another Japanese view of communication, purposefully cultivated by Japanese men in particular, is *haragei.* Nearly impossible to translate, *haragei* has been variously rendered as "belly communication," "stomach art," or "belly language," the stomach being the traditional center of man's being and emotions. Like *ishin-denshin,* it is communication that is indirect, suggestive, and allusive. It is communication that relies, in part, on the intuition and understanding of the receiver—and the communicator's talent and skill in ascertaining what the receiver is capable of understanding. In the context of business negotiations between the talented and experienced, *haragei* adds to *ishin-denshin* a competitive aspect and may be likened to a contest between grand champions in chess. Communication is slow, sometimes almost wordless. The "moves" depend upon skill in sythesizing everything that you know about the other person and everything that you know he knows about you. In such a competitive context, you do not reveal the essence of what is in your *hara* ("belly"), but you manage to make your purpose and intention known.

The cornerstone of both *ishin-denshin* and *haragei* is an ancient, homogeneous, and insular culture. The older generation is sometimes heard to say that the new generation has lost its "*ishin-denshin* ability" because it is out of touch with tradition.

In contrast, Americans live in a land where people speak different languages, belong to different races and religions, and are more often than not children or grandchildren of immigrants. In such a cultural hotch-potch, notions of "nonverbal" communication are quaint—and impracticable. America's variety of peoples is reflected in a verbal richness upon which Americans depend to be understood. Living in a heterogeneous society, Americans must speak, and speak loudly and clearly, with their tongues, in order to communicate with one another. Given these polar differences, it is not surprising that communication between Japanese and Americans requires patience and diligent study of one another's worlds.

Table of Contents

PART I
FOUNDATIONS

Part I focuses on fundamental tenets of Japanese culture, some of which are utterly alien to most Americans and others of which are antithetical to American assumptions and norms. An understanding of what motivates the characteristic behavior of Japanese businesspeople is essential to effective communication with them.

Equally important is an understanding of the typical range of individual differences. The degree of adherence to Japanese norms is based on factors such as individual experience and the setting in which the individual is operating. The best chance of understanding what Japanese businesspeople do and say occurs when an understanding of their culture and of their individual differences coincides.

1 Understanding Your Japanese Audience

F.O.B.S VERSUS S.O.B.S

The cardinal rule of effective communication is to know your audience, be it an individual or a group. Of course, the more you know about your audience, that is, the more facts at your disposal that differentiate a particular audience from all other audiences, the more effectively you will be able to make yourself understood in a way that your audience can accept.

Without giving the matter much conscious thought, we habitually tailor both the style and substance of our communications to the audience. We coo at babies, but not at ambassadors. We save off-color jokes for close friends whom we know will not be offended. A computer salesperson who hopes to sell a computer to a poet who has never owned one (is well advised to) speak slowly and avoid technical jargon. In effect, we regularly "translate" to a mode that we hope will be both comprehensible and inoffensive to the receiver of the communication.

Within the larger "audience" of all Japanese businesspeople, there are discrete audiences with which it is advisable to become familiar. To be sure, 90 percent of the Japanese businesspeople you are likely to meet will wear dark, conservative business suits, play golf, and sport expensive accessories. However, despite similarities in appearance, Japanese businesspeople today span a far wider range of experience and sophistication than was the case 20 years ago. At one end of the spectrum are what might be called the F.O.B.s, short for "Fresh Off the Boat." At the other are what might be described as the S.O.B.s, short for "Seasoned Old Boys." The ability to communicate effectively with either group requires some understanding of their respective backgrounds and the ability to differentiate between them.

A display of appropriate Japanese etiquette or the right word or gesture to convey a typically Japanese sentiment will not be forgotten and may be positively rewarded even years later.

F.O.B.s are closer to the stereotypical view some Americans still hold of Japanese. Usually they are in their fifties or older. They are as likely as not to have spent their formative years in the countryside where traditional Japanese values have always been strongest. In 1945, when World War II ended, more than half the Japanese population resided in agricultural communities. Thus, Japanese in their fifties or older completed their primary schooling in the countryside. Chances are that their parents and grandparents were farmers. At the beginning of their careers, they probably never imagined that they would be required as part of their jobs to venture out of Japan. Naturally, they are ill equipped emotionally and linguistically to deal with anything non-Japanese. They tend to feel ill at ease and perhaps even intimidated when out of Japan, and often must depend totally upon their interpreters, younger colleagues, or the members of their branch offices in major U.S. cities. It is this group of Japanese who would most appreciate and be favorably impressed by your demonstrating an understanding of things Japanese. A display of appropriate Japanese etiquette or the right word or gesture to convey a typically Japanese sentiment will not be forgotten and may be positively rewarded even years later.

At the other extreme are the S.O.B.s. In its "pure form," this type is worldly and sophisticated and probably travels between Japan and the rest of world several times each year. This cosmopolitan Japanese may have had a succession of foreign postings, may have attended a graduate program in an American business school and, in addition to speaking fluent English, probably has studied one or two additional foreign languages. An S.O.B. is as comfortable discussing Mozart and American football teams as he is attending a *koto* concert or a *sumo* match. In fact, some S.O.B.s have lived in the United States or other Western countries so long that reentry into Japanese society is traumatic both for them and their families.

No prominent M.B.A. program in the United States lacks a significant contingent of Japanese students. Generally dispatched by organizations for which they have worked for at least several years, they have been recognized as the cream of the Japanese corporate crop and are S.O.B.s in training. At Northwestern University's Kellogg Graduate School of Management, rated as the number one M.B.A. program in the United States by *Business Week* in each of the past few years, more than 250 Japanese applied for a total of 370 places available in 1991. Twenty-nine Japanese students were enrolled during the 1990–91 academic year.

Of course, nearly all Japanese businesspeople you are likely to encounter fall somewhere in between these "ideal" types. "Ideal" here is used in the sociological sense of providing an abstract model. Of course, reality only rarely displays the ideal type. Nevertheless, what is effective with a more traditional Japanese may not be effective with a more cosmopolitan Japanese, and vice versa. A gesture of appreciation communicated in the form of a dinner at the most exclusive French restaurant in town would be lost on a very traditional Japanese for whom heavy French sauces could pose a positive hardship. On the other hand, you will not impress an S.O.B. by taking him to a Japanese restaurant with nothing particular to distinguish it.

PLACE

Both S.O.B.s' and F.O.B.s' expectations and behavior may change depending on whether they are operating on their own turf, on your turf, or as is becoming increasingly common, in a neutral third place.

When a Japanese businessperson, whether F.O.B. or S.O.B., is in an American's office in the United States, his mind-set is that he is in less familiar territory. As such, he is likely to be more open to new experiences and more tolerant of deviations from the way he is used to being treated. The lack of an appropriate bow from an American host is likely to be better accepted than it would be if the meeting were taking place in his Tokyo office. Acceptance may be even more forthcoming from F.O.B.s, who expect that all foreigners by definition behave very strangely, than by S.O.B.s, who may expect that an American host will have at least some sophistication and familiarity with Japanese business etiquette.

The same Japanese businessperson who willingly tolerates otherwise offensive behaviors when they occur in a foreign setting is probably less willing to accept a breach of Japanese etiquette or a display of "un-Japanese" values that occurs on his home turf, especially if his colleagues are present and the particular "offense" committed by the foreigner causes him to "lose face."

Nowadays meetings frequently take place on neither party's home turf, but in a convenient city that is the home of neither, such as Singapore, Hong Kong, London, or Paris. In a neutral setting, both parties may be more open minded as to their cultural differences—or both may insist that things be done "my way."

The key point in all this is that the same individual has different expectations and behaves differently depending upon the setting. As a communicator, it is wise to gauge the effect that the setting may be having on your particular audience.

A ROSE IS NOT A ROSE IS NOT A ROSE

The third reason that a list of bare do's and don'ts offers insufficient guidance in communication with the Japanese business world is that a common maxim may be applied quite differently in each culture. For example, a stated principle in both Japan and the United States is that "the customer is king." However, the degree of adherence to the principle differs to such an extent in the two countries that the result is a qualitative difference in Japanese and American behavior. This is so because other cultural values mediate in situations involving vendors and customers. For example, as will be discussed in detail in Part II, Japan is a vertical society in which virtually every relationship is hierarchical. The rule that the customer is king fits nicely into the Japanese sense of hierarchy. The customer is *always* superior and calls the shots; the customer is never wrong.

One of us witnessed the following incident which occurred in Chicago's poshest Japanese restaurant: Several members of a Chicago law firm were hosting several executives employed by a potential Japanese client. When the food was delivered to the table, one of the junior American lawyers began immediately eating from a plate that was meant to have been delivered to the most senior Japanese visitor. The seasoned senior partner in the American law firm, understanding exactly what had happened, nevertheless complained to the maitre d', in Japanese, "You have not brought my honored guest what he ordered." An equally knowing and willing conspirator to the "cover-up" of the junior American lawyer's mistake, the maitre d' humbly apologized for and rectified the "error."

By contrast to Japan, America is, at least aspirationally, an egalitarian society. So while it may make good marketing sense in the United States to provide customers with service better than that of a competitor, unlike as in Japan, no seller or salesperson is expected to behave as if the customer is actually in the position of a superior holding unassailable prerogatives.

An everyday example of the difference is available in comparing what typically happens at closing time in an American and in a Japanese retail store. In the United States, as much as 10 or 15 minutes before closing, cash registers begin to be closed down and clerks begin to prepare for their departure. If a customer seeks assistance 5 minutes before closing, a clerk may be palpably annoyed at the customer's lack of sensitivity to the fact that the clerk has a personal life to attend to that is certainly no less important than the customer's need for a pair of socks. On the other hand, a customer who walks into a retail store in Japan even 1 minute before closing fully expects to transact business even if it requires the clerk to stay late. Regardless of true feelings, the clerk never displays annoyance but behaves as though it is his or her good fortune to have the opportunity to serve the last customer of the day; the clerk responds to the customer's final departure with a deep bow. To an American steeped in the tradition of Jacksonian democracy, the clerk's behavior may be viewed as bordering on being degrading.

In order, then, to be able to communicate effectively with Japanese in the myriad circumstances that no practical guide can fully cover, it is necessary to know the principles of Japanese culture, for they provide the intellectual tools to analyze new situations. That is, the reader will acquire the ability to interpret meaning and respond accordingly in varying circumstances. We turn now to those principles.

2 A Homogeneous Island Nation

Americans and Japanese share many aspirations, especially material ones. Things that members of both groups hope to achieve in their lives include economic security and career success (at least for Japanese males). Like Americans, Japanese want comfortable homes and a good education for their children. Nevertheless, it would be a grave mistake to assume that because Japanese and Americans may seek the same outcomes, they function in society and in business basically the same way.

The United States occupies a large fraction of an entire continent and is peopled by groups originating in every corner of the earth, by individuals of every race and of every religion. By contrast, Japan is an island nation whose population is among the most homogeneous in the world. This single, terribly obvious statement either explains or is related to nearly everything there is to know about Japanese culture. Moreover, regardless of any other change that could even theoretically occur in either Japanese or American society, it is a virtual certainty that Japan will remain overwhelmingly homogeneous.

YAMATO RACE

Homogeneity makes itself felt in almost every aspect of Japanese culture and society. Most striking is the racial and ethnic homogeneity of the citizenry. Ninety-nine percent of Japanese belong to the "Yamato race," which is their alternate way of referring to the Japanese people. Every member of the Yamato race is aware of the mythology that they share a single, common ancestor called Amaterasu. In the period before and during World War II, when nationalistic militarism prevailed, the belief in a single, common ancestor was heavily promoted by the authorities.

The Japanese government's candid unwillingness to permit more than a token number of Vietnamese boat people to settle in Japan is but one example of a policy decision that maintains Japan's racial and ethnic homogeneity.

Only a smattering of Japanese citizens, 3,000 to 4,000, are pure aboriginals of Northern Japan, racially distinct from the Yamatos of the South. Another 600,000 are of Korean ancestry, several 10,000 are of Chinese ancestry, and a handful are of Western origin.

This racial and ethnic homogeneity is certainly not entirely a function of Japan's circumstance as an island nation. Origin resides in geography, but geography has been followed by policy. It is extremely difficult for non-Japanese to become citizens of Japan. Unlike in the United States, where any person born on United States soil is automatically entitled to citizenship, the general rule in Japan is that entitlement to Japanese citizenship depends upon one's father's being a Japanese citizen. The Japanese government's candid unwillingness to permit more than a token number of Vietnamese boat people to settle in Japan is but one example of a policy decision that maintains Japan's racial and ethnic homogeneity.

Another policy, less known to Americans, is that Koreans, even those born in Japan whose families have lived there for generations, are required to undergo an investigation and adopt Japanese names in order to obtain Japanese citizenship. Until 1992, when a new law becomes effective, adult Korean residents who have not become citizens of Japan are required to be fingerprinted. They can be deported if they break the law. The sentiment captured in the inscription on the American Statue of Liberty that invites the world's sundry poor, hungry, and tired to America's shores is not one that is readily understood in Japan.

Nothing in the preceeding discussion, however, should be confused with the concept of hospitality, which applies to the treatment of guests. As a general rule, Japanese are extremely, even extravagantly, hospitable. Japanese hospitality extends to foreigners.

HISTORICAL ISOLATION

Japan's history has been marked by an isolation unparalleled in Asia or in Europe. Separated from the Asian land mass, Japan had never been occupied by any other nation until 1945. The Japanese repelled two Mongol invasions during the thirteenth century and believed that they were saved by the intervention of the "divine wind," or *kamikaze*. Apparently the failed invasions were mounted during typhoon season, and the Mongols, not traditionally a seafaring people, were turned back by cataclysmic winds. As a result, foreign influence was relatively minimal, and the Japanese had an unfettered sense of shared history even before Japan developed a strong central government.

By contrast, development in Korea and China was immeasurably less coherent, not only because those nations were occupied by foreigners, but even more so because no occupying force conquered them in their entirety for any extended period. Accordingly, various regions developed differently from one another. To this day, regional identities are stronger in those countries than they are in Japan.

LINGUISTIC UNIFORMITY

Closely allied to racial, ethnic, and historic homogeneity is linguistic homogeneity. Despite the existence of numerous dialects for which Japanese retain acknowledged affection, nearly everyone is capable of communicating in standard Japanese. Standard Japanese is taught in every school and is the only language acceptable in the broadcast media. Furthermore, the Japanese language has had few grammatical changes, and until the postwar period, when wholesale introduction of American English vocabulary occurred, had assimilated only a small number of words from other languages. The single, dramatic exception was the adoption of a modified version of the Chinese writing system and concurrent assimilation of Chinese vocabulary beginning in the sixth century. The result of this linguistic homogeneity is that a ninth grader can see something, whether written in a book or inscribed on a stone as early as the tenth century and make sense of it. Even the distant past and its traditions are readily accessible.

RELIGIOUS HOMOGENEITY

Japan's religious homogeneity is both a cause and an effect of its ethnic, historical, and linguistic homogeneity. Buddhism, transformed into a Japanese version quite distinct from the Buddhism in other Asian countries, was voluntarily adopted by the ruling class. No invader's religion overcame the unifying force of Japanese Shintoism and Buddhism—and none was allowed to. Although the Portuguese established a beachhead in western Japan in the sixteenth century, their practice of the Jesuit religion was outlawed by 1630. Today, 98 percent of Japanese call themselves both Buddhists and Shintoists. Neither religion purports to be exclusive, and their tenets are viewed as governing different aspects of human experience. The majority of Japanese, however, to the extent that they practice their religion at all, practice it in a secularized rather than in a devotional way. They participate in ritual in much the same way as Americans might go on an Easter egg hunt or prepare Thanksgiving dinner. In a book that became a best-seller in Japan in the 1970s called *Japanese and the Jews*,[1] author Isaiah Ben Dasan hypothesized that the real universal religion in Japan is *Nihon-kyo*, which might be best translated as "Japanism." Ben Dasan found a comparable blurring of the distinction between religion and ethnicity among many Jews who find no contradiction in describing themselves as being both Jewish and atheist.

EDUCATIONAL UNIFORMITY

Another linchpin of Japanese homogeneity is the fact that everyone in Japan has had essentially the same education through high school. The Japanese constitution provides that every Japanese must have nine years of education: six years of elementary school and three years of middle school. Today more than 80 percent of Japanese also complete high school. The curriculum is prescribed by the national Ministry of Education and is identical everywhere in the country to the point that at any given week of the school year, sixth graders in Tokyo are likely to be studying the same math lesson as sixth graders in Okinawa. Uniformity in quality is enhanced by government subsidies to equalize teachers' pay in all regions of the country.

Admission to university is governed strictly by examination, and the high school curriculum is naturally closely tailored to maximize the opportunity to succeed in passing the examination. The system has been criticized as promoting conformity over creativity and original thinking. On the other hand, employers are assured that high school graduates are uniformly literate and have necessary computational skills regardless where they attended school.

There is simply no such thing as a high school graduate who cannot read a newspaper or fill out an employment application form.

---

[1]Isaish Ben Dasan, *Japanese and the Jews,* Weatherhill, Tokyo, 1981.

The system has been criticized as promoting conformity over creativity and original thinking. On the other hand, employers are assured that high school graduates are uniformly literate and have necessary computational skills regardless where they attended school.

SHARED INFORMATION

Japanese as a group also share the same information. There are three general newspapers distributed nationwide, each of which has a daily circulation (when morning and evening editions are totaled) of over 5 million. By contrast, *The New York Times*, the largest national circulation newspaper in the United States, has only slightly over 1 million subscribers. A copy of any one of these national newspapers is available by six o'clock in the morning in every town, village, and hamlet from Hokkaido in the north to Okinawa in the south. Their news and interpretation of events does not vary much from one to the other. For economic news, the *Nihon Keizei Shimbun*, the functional equivalent of *The Wall Street Journal*, is equally available throughout the country. In addition, broadcasts of NHK, Nihon Hoso Kyokai ("the Japan Broadcasting Corporation"), which is the Japanese national network much like the BBC in Britain, are available in the most remote reaches of the countryside. They are is also available by satellite network in many places abroad for the convenience of Japanese business travelers. The result of this commonality in the Japanese mass media is that a population of nearly 125 million possesses virtually identical information.

ECONOMIC HOMOGENEITY

Finally, Japanese are far more economically homogeneous than Americans. Income is much more evenly distributed in Japan than in any other noncommunist, highly industrialized society. The overwhelming majority of Japanese consider themselves middle class. High level executives are paid a fraction of the compensation of the captains of American industry.

However, there are unmistakable fissures in the Japanese sense of economic homogeneity, although as many as 90 percent of Japanese still identify themselves as middle class in response to surveys. The inequity resulting from a 262 percent increase in Tokyo land prices since 1985 has caused definite strains by creating a class of fabulously wealthy landowners. *Business Week* reported the case of a Tokyo resident whose home on the city's outskirts increased in value from $375,000 in 1986 to $1.25 million in 1990. This "middle-class" Japanese had borrowing power of over $900,000 based on nothing more than home ownership.[2] Before the huge acceleration in land prices, career employees could expect to be able to purchase an apartment or a home at the time of retirement. This is no longer the case. Nowadays, one of the most attractive characteristics of a potential marriage partner is ownership of real estate.

The Japanese themselves refer to the negative aspects of their perceived uniqueness as *shimaguni konjo* or "island nation mentality."

ISLAND NATION MENTALITY

All these sources of homogeneity combine to create a strong sense of uniqueness that in some circumstances has served the Japanese well, but has also made them something of an anomaly in today's international community where they are viewed in certain quarters as ethnocentric or even xenophobic, having at once a disregard for the merits of other cultures and a sense of trepidation at having to interact with foreigners. The Japanese themselves refer to the negative aspects of their perceived uniqueness as *shimaguni konjo* or "island nation mentality."

On the positive side of this sense of shared destiny is the relative ease with which Japanese can work in unity. Comparing the Japanese with the American response to the necessity of conserving gasoline during the oil crises of 1973 and 1979, is illustrative: While many Americans adhered to the 55 mile per hour speed limit, others violated the law flagrantly, especially in western and rural areas, and where it was felt that Washington had little understanding of or sympathy for the hardship of driving long distances in lonely places. In Japan, no law aimed at gasoline

---

[2]Business Week, April 23, 1990, p. 51.

conservation was necessary; a well-publicized campaign to conserve by slowing down and not driving private automobiles unnecessarily sufficed. National policy was almost universally observed without the existence of any sanction beyond, perhaps, the fear, very strong among the Japanese, of shame if one were observed disregarding conservation measures.

Another small, but telling, example of Japanese willingness to respond to what is perceived in the collective good is the following: The Ministry of Health and Welfare at one point decided that the word *ronen*, which means "old age," had a negative connotation and sponsored a contest to find a better word to refer officially to old people. Over 3 million Japanese responded with suggestions! The winning word was *jukunen*, which means "seasoned" or "ripened age."

HIGH-CONTEXT CULTURE

The critical implication of Japanese homogeneity as it respects communicating with the Japanese business community is that, among themselves, Japanese businesspeople do not feel a need to spell out every detail. They belong to what cultural anthropologists call a "high-context culture." By contrast, American businesspeople operate in a relatively low-context culture.

A high-context culture is homogeneous to the point that meaning is communicated as much through the context of the communication as through the content. The ideal means of communication in a high-context culture is reflected in *ishin-denshin* and *haragei*.

By contrast, low-context cultures, such as American culture, are usually heterogeneous. Meaning must be communicated principally through content because context is an unreliable indicator of what somebody else who is in a different group, for example, a different race, religion, level of education, and class means. The concept of written contract flourishes in a low-context culture; every contingency must be anticipated because there is no source of guidance, other than the contract itself, to ascertain what the parties meant. On the other hand, in the high-context Japanese culture, spelling out every contingency may be considered an insulting display of mistrust.

A potent illustration of the difference between a "high-context" and "low-context" response to a potential deal is illustrated by a scene from the authors' marriage. Many years ago, a Japanese television network approached Hiroki with a proposal to make our family the subject of a television documentary. Joan's initial enthusiasm for the project was shattered when she learned that the deal had been struck without any mention of the amount of remuneration for having four cameramen following the family around for a week. True to Hiroki's prediction, when the filming was completed, the Japanese producer left a gratuity in a very appropriate amount for the family's week of service. As Hiroki insisted, it would be unthinkable for as large and respected an organization as a major network not to provide compensation appropriate for the project. Therefore, discussion of compensation was unnecessary, if not downright impolite. Joan to this day wonders whether Hiroki was right or merely lucky.

Another phenomenon associated with communication in high-context culture such as Japan's is the expectation that one's appropriate needs and desires will be anticipated and met without the embarrassing necessity of having to state them. Without the exchange of a single word, a business visitor will be brought refreshments, a car will be waiting, a helper will appear to carry a heavy package, and the like. An F.O.B. will not be placated by a statement such as "Oh, you should have told me that you needed a taxi." Even an S.O.B. may not be entirely happy about having to ask.

3 From *Amae* to *Tatemae*

Having explored the premise that Japan is a homogeneous island nation, it is necessary to examine those Japanese cultural phenomena that directly impact communication.

AMBIGUITY

Unlike most Westerners, Japanese are comfortable with ambiguity. In fact, in many situations Japanese embrace ambiguity and apparent indecisiveness because they are thought to enhance the fulfillment of other cherished goals such as face (its preservation) and harmony. By contrast, Westerners are most at home with a clear cut "yes" or "no," "right" or "wrong," "here" or "there." Hesitation to make a choice where a clear dichotomy presents itself is considered indecisive, and indecisiveness tends to be viewed as a negative trait, especially in corporate life.

For Japanese, reality is less a series of mutually exclusive choices and more a continuum of innumerable points. The Japanese are not very comfortable in describing a phenomenon in terms that designate an extreme, such as "success" or "failure," "wonderful" or "terrible," "love" or "hate." When they do hear such expressions, they assume that the speaker means them to be taken literally. If someone at the table in a restaurant responds to the question "How's your food?" with "It's terrible," a Japanese listener is likely to understand that the food is genuinely unfit for human consumption. The Japanese penchant to see things in relative rather than absolute terms is reflected in their use of three, rather than two, sets of demonstrative pronouns and adjectives. In English, it is possible only to speak of "this" or "that," translated into Japanese as *kore* and *are*, respectively. Japanese have a third pronoun, *sore* which designates an intermediate position from the speaker's point of view.

> **... forcing a Japanese business person to go on record with statements embodying clear directives or even clear preferences may cause him discomfort. Americans try to please others by giving them what they want. On the other hand, Japanese endeavor to please others by not risking the expression of a wish if there is the remotest chance that the other person will be unable to fulfill it.**

The Japanese view of the world in relative rather than absolute terms is reflected in Japanese art and architecture as well as in habits of communication. For example, traditional Japanese buildings do not have a line of demarcation between indoors and outdoors. Rather, a significant fraction of the limited space available is dedicated to an intermediate area between "in" and "out" that can be fully or partially opened depending upon the dictates of season and circumstance. The same disinclination to create dichotomies occurs in traditional Japanese painting. The painter does not feel compelled to fill the entire canvas in order to fix the boundary between life and art. Similarly, Japanese law and custom avoid results in which one party is declared right and the other unequivocally wrong. For example, concepts such as mediation and no-fault divorce that have recently taken hold in the United States have always been the norm in Japan.

Because of the quality of ambiguity in Japanese verbal communication, Americans sometimes find Japanese altogether too tentative. However, forcing a Japanese business person to go on record with statements embodying clear directives or even clear preferences may cause him discomfort. Americans try to please others by giving them what they want. On the other hand, Japanese endeavor to please others by not risking the expression of a wish if there is the remotest chance that the other person will be unable to fulfill it.

The reason is that Japanese strive to save the other person's face and to promote the harmony that otherwise would be disturbed.

An everyday, but not atypical example of working at culturally grounded cross-purposes occurs when an American host tries to encourage a Japanese guest to express what he wants: coffee or tea? cream or black? sugar or sweetener? this chair or that chair? window open or closed? What is viewed as solicitude by the American is felt as emotionally taxing by the Japanese. What if he expresses a preference for cream and the cream has run out, causing his host to lose face? His out in Japanese is to say *dotchidemo ii desu*—"anything is fine." However, such equivocation may seem strange and may be experienced as frustrating for the American trying his best to be accommodating.

In Japan, the individual is always subservient to the group. Personal convenience, personal choice, even personal liberty are simply not as important.

PRIMACY OF THE COLLECTIVITY

To the extent that the American brand of democracy depends upon the exaltation of the individual, the Japanese will never fully adopt it. In Japan, the individual is always subservient to the group. Personal convenience, personal choice, even personal liberty are simply not as important.

An individual is evaluated not in terms of his talents, but in terms of his ability to serve and to function effectively within the group. Japanese employers do not emphasize discrete skills or specific achievements in their hiring practices. Instead they hire the whole person, *marugakae*, or "lock, stock, and barrel." It is assumed that anyone who has gone through the uniform, rigorous hoops required for entry into a good university has the right stuff that can be molded to the company's specific needs at any given time. Once hired, new employees are apt to go through years of training, learning many aspects of the company's business rather than becoming experts in limited areas as quickly as possible. Thus, an employee's sense of identity resides in the collectivity rather than within the borders of his own personality. Nor is he possessed of any abstract moral code that takes precedence over the welfare of the group.

This overriding sense of group identity is reflected in the way in which Japanese refer to themselves. It may well explain why Japanese always state their family names first and why they introduce themselves as "Tanaka of Machida Corporation" or "Suzuki of Sumitomo" without stating whether they are the president of the company or the president's chauffeur. Americans, on the other hand, are more likely to introduce themselves as "My name is Joe Smith and I'm a chemical engineer." Organizational affiliation is somewhat of a secondary concern.

The degree of the sense of group affiliation is also reflected in what employees view as the scope of their responsibility. Generally, in an American setting an individual views responsibility as being associated with discrete tasks. Once assigned tasks are completed, an employee's responsibilities are fully discharged. He is "off duty" and reverts completely to his identity as an individual. For example, once a flight is over, the flight attendant's duties are complete. An American flight attendant who happens to be flying while off duty feels no sense of responsibility for the flight. However, a Japanese flight attendant in the same situation is much more apt to feel that, as a "member" of Japan Air Lines, his duties are neither strictly circumscribed by job description, nor limited to official on the job hours, but continue as long as a member of Japan Air Lines is needed on the scene, whether by passengers, other crew members, or just the general public. The authors had the opportunity to contrast the behavior of an American airport station manager employed by a major U.S. airline and his Japanese counterpart employed by Japan Air Lines. The authors were seeing off their 15-year-old son on a flight to Tokyo operated by the U.S. airline. They waited to watch the airplane depart from the gate after all the passengers had boarded. Instead of taxiing away, however, the airplane began to dump large amounts of fuel on the tarmac. Much to the authors' consternation, the airplane was soon sitting in a pool of jet fuel. Fire engines pulled up to the side of the airplane and began spreading foam. By this time, half crazed with anxiety, the authors searched, without success, for a representative of the airline able to explain what seemed like a potentially dreadful situation. Just as the authors' level of terror reached an intolerable level, the jumbo jet taxied away.

A few weeks later, the authors saw off passengers departing Chicago for Tokyo on Japan Air Lines. JAL's white-gloved station manager remained in the passenger area until all the passengers boarded the aircraft. He then stationed himself on the tarmac until the loading and fueling process was complete. Only when the plane taxied away did he salute and bow. When the plane was out of sight, he came back to the terminal.

KAO

A corollary of collective identity is the Japanese sense of *kao*, or "face." *Kao* embodies both one's personality and sense of self-worth. The slightest humiliation causes an immediate and sometimes irretrievable loss of one's *kao*.

Americans may be no happier about losing face than are Japanese. However, because of the strong sense of collectivity and the sense that collective expectations must be met, failure to fulfill those expectations causes much greater distress to Japanese. Attention being drawn to the failure can be intolerable.

Causing a loss of face will not often be forgiven. Never should you publicly criticize a Japanese. Necessary criticism should be private and subtle, and never left unmitigated by the absence of concurrent emphasis of a person's positive points and contributions to the group.

Placing a person squarely, however inadvertently, in a situation where he cannot fulfill your expectations will cause him to lose face. Requests should, therefore, be subtle and ambiguous so that if they remain unfulfilled, no one will lose face.

AMAE

Amae is the fundamental, uniquely Japanese psychological mechanism that in part explains the power of Japanese collectivism. *Amae* defies precise translation, but derives from the verb *amaeru*, which roughly means "to be sweet to someone." *Amae* describes an interdependence between two persons. *Amae* is thought positive and productive. Unlike in the West, in Japan psychological maturity us not viewed as the achievement of independence and autonomy. Rather, the single most important sign of maturity is a person's mastery of the mechanism of interdependence for productive purposes, including the cultivation of business relationships.

The model for *amae* in adult life is the *amae* between mother and infant. Japanese take it as a law of nature that a baby will *amaeru* to its mother and that the mother is always available to meet all the baby's needs without hesitation. A Japanese baby's physical contact with its mother is virtually constant. Cooking, shopping, and housework are ordinarily accomplished while a baby is carried in a sling on its mother's back. Maternal devotion and benevolence engender unbounded trust and are repaid with filial piety. As the child grows, its tie to the mother is expressed in obedience and in striving to meet the mother's expectations for the child's achievement. Later, school and ultimately business relationships are formed on the model of the prototypical *amae* between mother and child. Teachers and bosses offer benevolence and care to their students and subordinates in exchange for obedience. The same sense of *amae* operates between suppliers and purchasers, between manufacturers and wholesalers—and in practically any situation where someone, usually because of status, is by Japanese custom charged with the responsibility of caring for someone else.

WA

Wa, or "harmony," closely related to interdependence, is exalted by Japanese. The difference between *amae* and *wa* is that former applies to the psychology of interdependence in hierarchical relationships and the latter applies horizontally between members of a group or between groups. Japanese will go to great lengths to maintain *wa*, even with people they neither admire nor respect, so long as they know that their interaction must continue. Confrontation is abhorrent. To confront someone directly, or to provoke confrontation, is considered the height of immaturity. Once broken, *wa* is difficult to repair.

HONNE AND TATEMAE

Honne and *tatemae* are two distinct channels of verbal communication. Although difficult to translate accurately, *tatemae* roughly means "facade." *Tatemae* is formal or official communication. It is the speech of the public *personum*, the language of facade. *Honne* means "true voice." *Honne* is the language of the heart. It is unvarnished truth—and sometimes an expression of naked sentiment that may embarrass Americans.

In practically any culture, there are notable differences in public and private communications. However, in English, there are no specific words to identify and point up the distinction between them. In fact, Americans in many circumstances promote the fiction that they always say the same things in the same manner whether they are speaking publicly or privately. It does not comport with American values of openness and candor to acknowledge that what one says in public i*s expected* to be different from what one says in private. Japanese not only specifically acknowledge the difference between public and private speech and give them distinct names—they almost invariably adhere to rules that determine whether *honne* or *tatemae* is the appropriate mode of communication under given circumstances.

Japanese not only specifically acknowledge the difference between public and private speech and give them distinct names—they almost invariably adhere to rules that determine whether *honne* or *tatemae* is the appropriate mode of communication under given circumstances.

In offices, in groups during business hours, and most other times when statements are public, the only language spoken is *tatemae*. In *tatemae* speech, the speaker will go to whatever lengths are necessary to save his own as well as the listener's face. *Honne* typically takes its turn after office hours.

For example, a Japanese vendor who is asked in an official meeting whether he will be able to deliver goods at the time promised is likely to respond "we'll do our best," or "I certainly hope so," even if he knows that he is unlikely to meet the delivery schedule agreed to. The same evening, the vendor may take his customer to a bar. After a few drinks, he may switch to *honne* and explain that certain unanticipated production problems will result in delivery being delayed. The *honne* conversation is unlikely ever to be referred to in subsequent conversations between the vendor and customer while they are speaking in the *tatemae* mode, but the customer can rely completely on what the vendor told him in the bar and can act on the information communicated with complete confidence.

To Americans, *honne/tatemae* distinctions may seem duplicitous. But Japanese feel neither two-faced nor dishonest. Rather, they believe that it is important to preserve *tatemae* in order to save the face of everyone involved and *honne* in order to operate effectively.

Of course, a prerequisite to communication in the *honne* mode is the prior development of a personal relationship. Such relationships are nurtured after business hours in Tokyo's innumerable eating and drinking establishments where Japanese businesspeople spend long hours. After-hours gatherings provide a setting for switching to the *honne* mode. Sometimes the transition to *honne* is marked by the expression *honne de ikimasho*, or "let's proceed by means of *honne*." Subordinates then are allowed to tell their bosses what they think without either party losing face. Of course, people from two different business organizations can also communicate in the *honne* mode after having laid the appropriate ground-work. What transpires during these gatherings, whether among members of the same business organization or between members of different business organizations, may be just as important as events during business hours where communication is almost always in the *tatemae* mode.

To Americans, *honne/tatemae* distinctions may seem duplicitous. But Japanese feel neither two-faced nor dishonest. Rather, they believe that it is important to preserve *tatemae* in order to save the face of everyone involved and *honne* in order to operate effectively.

Because Americans do not consciously make such clear distinctions between public and private modes of communication, they do not feel it necessary to establish close personal relationships with bosses and co-workers. Ordinarily, family and personal matters are not discussed with people at work. In the United States, friendship that develops because of a long standing work or business relationship is viewed as a usually acceptable, but certainly not necessary, outcome. In Japanese business organizations, no clear distinction is made between what is personal and what is work related.

Americans sometimes feel frustrated and impatient with what they view as the inordinate amount of time Japanese spend on establishing relationships. They may wonder what was supposed to have been the purpose of a meeting lacking any apparent agenda other than what they may view as a stilted conversation about the respective hobbies and families of those present. They may even find the after-hours drinking and singing tiresome or even childish. However, these encounters are anything but meaningless to the Japanese. They are instead the opportunity to establish the kind of relationship that Japanese deem essential to doing business effectively. If an American wishes to hear his Japanese counterpart's "true voice," such "meetings" are indispensable.

ON AND *GIRI*

Although Americans may not have specific words for *honne* and *tatemae*, the phenomena they represent is not terribly foreign to Americans. On the other hand, *on* and *giri* are less familiar concepts.

On can be used to great effect by Americans dealing with Japanese. If a Japanese receives a favor worthy of engendering *on*, he will try to repay the kindness for the rest of his life.

Both *on* and *giri* refer to duties and obligations, but of two very different types. *Giri* is a type of obligation that one acquires simply by status. A Japanese man owes *giri* to the person who marries his sister simply because he has become a member of the family. Whether he likes or even has met his brother-in-law in person is irrelevant. The brother-in-law is owed any help he needs within reason and is obliged to repay it within reason. Similarly, *giri* is owed anyone who works for the same company. Duties performed and favors given as a result of *giri* are straightforward, even sometimes perfunctory, and can and must be repaid.

On the other hand, *on* can never be repaid. *On* makes a permanent "debtor" out of the beneficiary. The obligation of *on* arises as a result of a favor that the beneficiary did not have coming to him on account of *giri*; it is a favor that goes beyond the call of static duty in a situation where someone has rendered particular benevolence, mercy, or assistance during a trying time or regarding a crucial matter. The prototype of all *on* is the obligation that Japanese children feel toward their parents who are viewed as not only having given them life, but tended selflessly to their every need.

On can be used to great effect by Americans dealing with Japanese. If a Japanese receives a favor worthy of engendering *on*, he will try to repay the kindness for the rest of his life. The favor may be something as simple as helping to get a Japanese expatriate's son enrolled in an American school, or hosting a Japanese exchange student, or helping to find the right medical specialist when someone is ill. While these kindnesses may not seem extraordinary in American eyes, they may engender overwhelming gratitude in Japanese, especially in F.O.B.s. If the Japanese who feels *on* toward you happens to be your customer, don't be surprised is he continues to buy from you even if your price is not quite as good as your competitors'.

Since *on* can be such a valuable commodity, it is not surprising that people sometimes try to "sell *on*." The Japanese expression for selling *on* is *on o uru*. Bob Greene, a syndicated columnist at *The Chicago Tribune* related that he once spent three days showing two Japanese around Chicago. The Japanese absolutely insisted that they pick up the entire tab at every single meal regardless how much he protested. Bob Greene may not have realized he was the target of *"on* selling."

It is most important that Americans doing business with Japanese be able to recognize whether a Japanese is acting out of *on* or *giri*. An understanding of which is which provides the basis for seizing opportunities to establish virtually permanent relationships as well as to avoid unrealistic expectations.

OMOIYARI AND ENRYO

Omoiyari means "showing consideration" and *enryo* means "holding back" when consideration is shown to you. *Enryo* generally occurs in the *tatemae* mode of communication.

Japanese demonstrate their *omoiyari* by anticipating the needs of others and fulfilling those needs without comment before being asked. On a hot summer's day in Japan, a guest will be brought a bottle of cold beer that has already been opened before any words are exchanged regarding refreshments. A car will be ordered and waiting for an important business visitor without any discussion of transportation. Of course, sometimes a visitor will have hired his own car, and the car hired by the company he is visiting will have been for naught. Japanese, however, do not consider this wasteful, but as an ordinary cost of doing business.

Americans do not so much anticipate the needs of those to whom they wish to show consideration but solicit requests and strive to fulfill them. Many Japanese, but especially F.O.B.s, experience typical American questions as to what they want as a somewhat crude lack of *omoiyari*.

American reaction to Japanese *omoiyari* is apt to be ambivalent. The following question was posed to a large group of experienced American flight attendants: "Which passengers are more difficult to serve, Japanese or Americans?" The group's illuminating response was split approximately 50–50. Those who felt that Japanese passengers were easier to handle said it was because they rarely make demands on the flight attendant. Those who found Japanese passengers more difficult to serve said it was because they could never tell what the Japanese want.

As an American business visitor to Japan, you can sometimes calculate where you stand by evaluating the degree of *omoiyari* shown to you. Have you been met at the airport by a high-ranking manager despite your knowing perfectly well how to get around in Tokyo? Has anyone escorted you to the street after a business meeting and waited until your car was driven away?

While a show of virtuous *omoiyari* is the reason a company will hire a car for its important visitors, a virtuous show of *enryo* sometimes explains why the visitor hired his own car. It also explains why the only appropriate adult reaction when receiving a gift in Japan is to say "Oh, I don't deserve this." The recipient graciously accepts the gift only after the giver proffers it a second time. Similarly, the recipient of an invitation must decline at least once, no matter how much he would like to accept the invitation, in order to demonstrate *enryo*. Only after being pressed a second time will he feel comfortable in accepting.

Because of *enryo*, it is important that an invitation to a Japanese be repeated at least twice if it is meant to be accepted. By the same token, an invitation that is not meant to be accepted can be safely extended once—except to S.O.B.s—without fear of incurring an unwanted obligation.

EMOTIONS

Japanese have a deserved reputation for hiding their emotions except when drinking and for being less than jovial or gregarious. Reserve is a cultivated trait among Japanese who may be consciously or unconsciously imbued with the Buddhist belief in the cyclical nature of the universe. If things appear to be one way now, it is certain that they will appear to be different later. A person happy at this moment is sure to be less happy the next. On the other hand, for one in despair, things can only change for the better.

Japanese generally subscribe to the principle that, over the long haul, human beings manage better if they do not readily give expression to transitory emotions. Maturity is thought to be reflected in mastering reserve. The authors overheard their young Japanese cousin's statement, "I'm so happy!" met with her mother's terse admonition not to say "such stupid things." Similarly, when a Japanese parent is congratulated on a child's outstanding achievement, the parent is likely to respond by saying, "It was just luck," or "we didn't know she had any ability," even though the parent may be bursting with pride.

Sometimes feelings are difficult to suppress, and the effort itself may seem strange to Westerners. For example, Japanese sometimes giggle to mask strong emotions. While relating the tragic news of his daughter's serious illness and his hope that she would survive, a Japanese friend of the authors could not help occasionally laughing as his sadness nearly overcame him.

Japanese sometimes do not know what to make of American expressiveness. They are apt to misinterpret completely the level of an American's feeling. For example, what might be a mild expression of annoyance by an American, such as "this is really driving me crazy," may be taken literally by a Japanese. As is often the case, the degree of misunderstanding may depend on whether the Japanese is an S.O.B. or an F.O.B.

To summarize,

1. Japanese are uncomfortable when forced to make their preferences clearly known.

2. Japanese view the scope of an employee's responsibility as being much wider than do Americans.

3. Unlike Americans, Japanese view psychological maturity as the mastery of interdependence.

4. Japanese scrupulously avoid any comment or action that causes the loss of face.

5. Japanese acknowledge and separate private and public communication.

6. Japanese divide duties into those that are perfunctory and those that arise from an extraordinary favor.

7. Japanese strive to fulfill the needs of others before being asked.

8. In Japan, hiding emotions is a sign of maturity.

4 Operating on Japanese Time

Culture determines how we apprehend time. A person's sense of time strongly influences behaviors associated with the organization and performance of work. Not surprisingly, Japanese and Americans do not necessarily share the same perceptions of time. In order to understand how Japanese businesspeople approach and execute tasks, it is necessary to understand Japanese perceptions of time.

MONOCHRONIC VERSUS POLYCHRONIC

Anthropologists have observed that there are two contrasting paradigms that reflect a human being's sense of time: polychronic and monochronic. A person with a monochronic sense of time perceives that time moves forward on a single track. A monochronic individual tends to apportion units of time to discrete tasks, estimates in advance the amount of time that each task is expected to occupy, and attempts to complete the task within the time allotted to it. A sense of accomplishment is derived from finishing each scheduled task.

A person with a polychronic sense of time does not preplan a series of tasks. Rather, a necessary task is attended to without being allotted any specific amount of time. If circumstances interfere with the completion of the task, it is temporarily abandoned. On the other hand, if a task is progressing unusually well, or for some other reason cannot be easily set aside, it is continued regardless of the time.

Obviously, a monochronic perception of time is most fitting in an urban, industrialized setting, while a polychronic sense of time is best suited to a society based on hunting or agriculture. An urban office worker performs tasks within an organization and must often interface with other people in his own or other organizations. As a result, working hours must be reasonably similar in all organizations. Meetings must be scheduled. Clients and customers must be dealt with at prearranged times. Deadlines must be met. Interruptions that derail schedules are perceived as annoying.

Such people see little value in setting rigid allotments of time for particular tasks. Things are simply allowed to take as long as they take.

By contrast, an Eskimo living in a traditional setting might get up in the morning and leave his dwelling to hunt walrus. If a storm develops, hunting is interrupted and he may return home to mend fishing nets. If the storm blows over, the net mending may be set aside and the hunt resumed. The shift from one "unfinished" task to another provokes no anxiety.

AMERICAN MONOCHRONISM VERSUS JAPANESE POLYCHRONISM

The United States' transformation from an economy based primarily on agriculture to a modern industrialized one took place at least one generation before the same transformation occurred in Japan. The majority of Americans have lived and worked for at least two generations in an urban environment. Most organize their work based on a monochronic sense of time. Business appointments are scheduled in advance, and schedules are generally adhered to. Of course, even the most meticulously planned schedules will be scrapped in the face of unexpected events, whether such events herald disaster or opportunity. However, the strong expectation is that tasks will be accomplished in a predetermined order within a pre-planned space of time. Deviations are allowed only for extremely compelling reasons, and when they occur, people tend to feel frustrated or overworked.

Japan as been urbanized and industrialized much more recently than the United States. There remains a strong residue of polychronism, particularly among those Japanese old enough to be current chieftains of business and industry. Such people see little value in setting rigid allotments of time for particular tasks. Things are simply allowed to take as long as they take.

There is no particular sense of frustration at the end of the day, even if the day continues well into the night, if a task has not been completed—as long as the process has been ongoing and things are moving in the right direction, however slowly. The Japanese sense of time coupled with the Japanese sense of loyalty to the company can result in a very long day indeed. This laissez-faire attitude toward time is particularly apparent when a project is in the planning stages.

Of course, neither model is consistently expressed in its "pure" form: Japanese make checklists and appointments which they are loathe to cancel, and Americans can lose themselves in a task and forget about the time. Nevertheless, an appreciation of these models has practical utility.

Many Japanese businesspeople will not understand why an American becomes restless after 6 P.M. on a Friday if a meeting is still in progress. They are likely to misinterpret an American's haste to "wrap things up" and start the weekend as a sign that the meeting is not going as well as it should. Likewise, many Japanese businesspeople will not comprehend why they are the recipients of a sudden "hard close," usually shortly before an American counterpart's scheduled departure from Narita.[1] The change in pace will seem incomprehensible and rude to the Japanese, and rather than getting things done in time, the American may find that things are not going to get done at all. In his book, *You Can Negotiate Anything*,[2] Herb Cohen points out the lack of wisdom in virtually any negotiating situation in letting your opponent know that you have a deadline, although the particular anecdote he relates has as its setting a negotiation between an American and a Japanese. The result of that negotiation was later viewed by the American as "the greatest Japanese victory since Pearl Harbor."

Certain obvious steps can be taken to minimize "time clashes." Avoid starting appointments with Japanese later than early afternoon and consider avoiding Fridays altogether if you want to spend your weekend away from your office. Always build more flexibility into a business trip to Japan to take advantage of an important last-minute invitation. Participating in a social event may not appear to advance your specific mission, but may pay huge dividends by cementing important relationships. In

---

[1]Named after the adjacent village which is now a growing city, Narita is the international airport that serves the eastern half of Japan's main island which includes the city of Tokyo.

[2]Herb Cohen, *You Can Negotiate Anything*, L. Stuart, Secaucus, New Jersey, 1980.

other words, always be prepared to spend an extra day to accept a golf invitation or to be a guest at someone's country house. Turning down such flattering invitations because of a sense that you must adhere to your departure schedule may not be cost effective.

TIMING AND DECISIONS

It has been observed that, at least throughout the 1970s, the time that it took for a Japanese business organization and an American business organization to get from the beginning to the end of a major project, such as developing and marketing a new product, or redesigning an automobile, were roughly equal. That is to say, no significant differences were found in the total time between the inception of an idea and its ultimate execution in business organizations in the two countries. However, what happens between these two points is remarkably different, so much so that involvement in common ventures can be a frustrating experience for both sides.

Typically, Americans feel that their Japanese counterparts move at a glacial pace—or not at all. However, in some instances, Americans found that Japanese moved full speed ahead in circumstances where the Americans were not yet prepared to move.

Why the discrepancies? The answers lie in the source of new ideas and the timing of decision making. For example, in an American company, a major decision such as going to market with a new product is typically made at a very early stage and involves a relatively small number of people. Ideas and decisions are the domain of high-ranking managers, usually at the senior vice president level or higher. Because of the small numbers and the high rank of the people involved at the earliest stages of an undertaking, a corporate decision may be reached within a few days or weeks. Thereafter, it may take considerable time in an American organization until the decision is actually implemented. The rest of the organization must be informed of the decision. Retooling may be necessary. A marketing and sales program has to be developed. In other words, only after the decision has been made are the "ponies" marshalled at the operational level.

By contrast, in a Japanese company most ideas are advanced by relatively low level employees. For example, among Japanese automakers as many as 90 percent of the ideas for change come from on-line workers and managers. Even lower-ranking employees of Japanese automakers drive the car that they produce and are, therefore, well positioned to suggest improvements. Logic and experience dictate that when an idea emanates from closer to the bottom of an organization, it takes longer for it to filter up to the level where major decisions are made. On its way to the top, the idea becomes known to most people in the operational sectors of the organization who have had time to consider and reconsider how to most effectively implement the idea. Accordingly, by the time a final decision to implement the idea is reached, the organization is poised to implement it quickly. The idea has already been examined and discussed in the research department, the marketing department, or whatever other department may be relevant to its implementation.

... among Japanese automakers as many as 90 percent of the ideas for change come from on-line workers and managers.

Given those differences, it should not be surprising that if Americans begin negotiating with the Japanese before an idea has been presented to the decision-making echelons of the Japanese organization, the Japanese will appear to be slow and indecisive. On the other hand, if Americans and Japanese first meet when upper management has already reached a decision to go ahead, the Japanese will almost inevitably be prepared to move more quickly than the Americans in executing the decision. In fact, in the past decade, Japanese have managed consistently to shorten the time for bringing out new products.

PLANNING AHEAD

As a general proposition, Japanese plan far longer in advance than do most Americans or Europeans. Japanese governmental and academic organizations tend to plan even farther ahead than Japanese business organizations. Trips abroad may be scheduled months or even years in advance.

For example, a professor at a Japanese university wrote to an American colleague at the University of Hawaii in the month of September to inform him that he would be arriving in Honolulu on Japan Air Lines' direct flight from Tokyo on October 27. The American professor met the flight to no avail. After confirming that his Japanese colleague had never boarded the flight, he took out the letter again and realized that his Japanese colleague was referring to October 27 of the following year.

Once a trip's route and agenda are fixed, Japanese tend to be rigid about sticking to plans. The kind of flexibility that Americans may describe as an ability to "wing it" is not considered a virtue among most mature Japanese who may be made to feel quite uncomfortable by frequent schedule changes.

This may seem to contradict earlier statements about monochronism versus polychronism. However, Japanese polychronism is much more compelling during planning stages than during execution. In some sense, every trip involves execution rather than pure planning. In addition, other forces may also be at work. Unlike Americans, the Japanese as a group did not become world travelers until after World War II and may feel less secure in unfamiliar environments.

PUNCTUALITY

Japanese sometimes appear to be slavishly punctual to Americans and even more so to other Asians. In fact, they are often observed to arrive 5 to 10 minutes early for appointments, sometimes to the embarrassment of their hosts. They maintain this punctuality at home as well as abroad even though extremely congested traffic conditions in Tokyo tend to made travel time uncertain. It is often advisable to take the subway or train rather than a limousine or taxi if you wish to ensure a punctual arrival. Although subways and trains can be extremely crowded, they run very frequently and stations are conveniently located. English language subway and train maps are available throughout the city.

The fact that Japanese are punctual despite the hardships of getting around in Tokyo demonstrates that punctuality is a cultural trait rather than a trait that is imposed purely by external realities. For example, in congested Bangkok, even businesspeople are habitually and unapologetically late. Arrival within half an hour of the appointed time generates little if any comment. By contrast, a Japanese who is even 10 minutes late is likely to apologize profusely.

Having asserted that the trait of being punctual has less to so with external exigencies and more to do with cultural norms, it should nevertheless be pointed out that there are very practical reasons for being on time in Japan. Because of the combination of population density and relative affluence, Japanese are forced to make arrangements months in advance to secure golf tee times, tennis courts, and even long-distance train tickets, especially during busy travel seasons. It is easy to understand why under such circumstances, you certainly risk drawing negative attention to yourself in Japan by being anything less than punctual.

To summarize,

1. The Japanese move slowly during the planning stages of projects and quickly after the planning has been completed and a decision made.

2. High-level people authorized to make decisions should be sent to meet with Japanese only if you know that a decision has already been reached by Japanese upper management. Otherwise, progress will be made more quickly if you send people at a functional level and exercise patience.

3. If you are meeting in the United States and wish to adhere to a typical American work schedule, scheduling appointments late in the day or on Fridays is to be avoided.

4. Unnecessary changes in schedules or agendas upset Japanese visitors. If a change must be made, carefully explain the nature of and reason for it.

5. The Japanese generally arrive a few minutes early; you must ensure your own punctuality in Japan.

6. A flexible departure date from Japan can offer opportunities for enhancement of business relationships.

5 Japanese Ageism, Sexism, and Racism

AGEISM

Japanese have traditionally regarded age as synonymous with wisdom. A person is accorded more respect simply by being older. The "ideal" Japanese family depicted in the media consists of three generations living under one roof. These days the ideal often goes unfulfilled. Adult children may be transferred by their employers to another city or even abroad where they establish separate households. Nevertheless, it is still considered somewhat shameful, if increasingly necessary, to place elderly relatives in nursing homes.

The Japanese regard for age is reflected in most large Japanese business organizations. However, as will be discussed shortly, the degree of systematic advantage for older employees may be diminishing.

In Japan, younger employees "pay their dues" in spades. Even those graduates of top national universities newly hired to be managers in prestigious companies or government ministries often live in crowded dormitories, work brutal hours, and spend months or years doing what similarly situated Americans would consider "scut work." The typical compensation system also demonstrates the equation of age with worth. Most mangers are given identical raises and bonuses at least until they are in their middle forties when they typically reach the rank of department head. It is only at this relatively late career stage that those who are elevated to positions in upper management begin to receive large increases in compensation. However, at the end of their careers, even those employees who were not destined to reach the top of the corporate ladder may be earning seven or more times the amount that they earned when they started their careers. The preference for seniority as the overwhelmingly significant factor in advancement means that the heads of major corporations are almost always in their sixties and that almost no one under 45 has unilateral power to make important decisions.

Since age is appreciated more than youth, many younger Japanese businesspeople try to project an image of maturity. Gray or balding heads do not breed much consternation in their owners. Young Japanese managers may practice speaking more slowly to affect the deliberateness that is supposed to accompany wisdom. They wear the most conservative clothing and sport accessories thought to be favored by the more mature, such as glasses whose frames are half tortoise shell and half wire.

Sometimes lacking full appreciation of Japanese ageism, American organizations have dispatched young superstars on important missions to Japan. Often these young emissaries fail miserably. Simply because of their youth, their mission may not be taken seriously by the Japanese.

Japanese have been particularly puzzled by the emissaries sent by certain states to head liaison offices in Japan. More than 30 states now have such offices. Because the positions do not pay very well, and because most Americans who have studied Japanese are relatively young, some Americans who have headed these liaison offices have been only in their twenties or thirties. Some have had a difficult time fulfilling their missions.

To avoid obstacles that a younger person may encounter in Japan, it is wise to send a mature manager to important meetings, even if the mature manager is not the most familiar with the details of the subject under discussion. A more junior person may, of course, go along to provide technical support and even do most of the talking.

While it is certainly the safer course to expect to encounter Japanese ageism, it may be diminishing to some extent. With every new generation, the older generation in Japan as elsewhere has been quick to complain that the younger generation is neither as disciplined nor as hard working. Nevertheless, since the beginning of the 1980s, Japanese have perceived that their generation gap is widening palpably. The term *shinjinrui*, which means "new human species," began to be commonly used to refer to those aspects of the younger generation that collectively represent a clear departure from tradition.

The *shinjinrui* were born in the 1960s in economic affluence. Most are college educated and some have even travelled abroad. They have read about or have seen how Westerners live and work and question whether their own work lives are unnecessarily grueling by comparison. They want more vacation and shorter working hours. They also question whether seniority should be rewarded more readily than talent and may resent marking time through the best years of their lives before having a chance to catch the brass ring. They may see greater rewards in working for small, high-tech companies or even foreign companies rather than for the Japanese corporate giants.

How widespread the current attitudes associated with the *shinjinrui* are remains to be seen. Certainly there are signs that at least a small percentage of S.O.B.s who have spent a significant portion of their early years abroad resist returning to the traditional corporate fold. Some even start their own companies. The jury is still out, however, as to whether a permanent diminution of Japanese ageism is in the offing.

The shift to a less ageist corporate culture, if it occurs, is not without well-known native harbingers who defied Japanese corporate ageism. The best known outside of Japan is Akio Morita, founder of Sony Corporation. In the 1950s, he was a young electrical engineer trying to start a business. Together with Masaru Ibuka, he founded his own company and recruited top engineering talent by promising compensation on the basis of merit rather than seniority. Others, less well known outside of Japan, whose success depended upon defying the traditional mold, are Soichiro Honda, who lacked even a high school education, and Kazuo Inamori, who quit college to found Kyoto Ceramics (Kyocera). Inamori has written of his own impatience with the system and is a strong critic of the slowness and ageism of the Japanese government bureaucracies. It is worth noting, however, that the companies established by these mavericks probably operate less differently from other Japanese corporations today than their beginnings might have indicated they would.

SEXISM

Japan's reputation as the most sexist society in the industrialized world is unfortunately justified. During the Meiji period, Japan borrowed Western technology and even, to a great extent, Western political structures. Never, however, has Japan embraced Western social attitudes.

Japan's business structure is still a man's world despite the fact that over half of adult Japanese women are part of the work force and about an equal number receive college degrees. The overwhelming percentage of Japanese working women are employed as seasonal, temporary, or part-time workers in relatively menial jobs. As a rule, they lack retirement or other employment benefits.

Women are present in corporate offices primarily as the ubiquitous O.L.s or "Office Ladies"—charming, uniformed young women who serve an interlude before marriage as receptionists, "gofers" and tea servers, and sometimes sentimentalized companions to older males in the company.

Even today only a handful of Japanese women occupy the management career tracks of major corporations or the powerful government bureaucracies, although an increasing number of companies, particularly in the financial services industry, are beginning to hire female college graduates in management training programs. However, even those who achieve career track positions are rarely afforded equal treatment. Americans have sometimes been embarrassed witnesses of the obsequious behavior of Japanese professional women in the presence of male colleagues. For several years we observed an extremely capable, hard-working Japanese female attaché in a Japanese consular office pouring tea for a succession of often less capable male colleagues.

In April 1988, Japan passed an equal employment law banning discrimination in hiring and pay. However, substantive change comes slowly. Employment advertisements seeking, for example, "male engineers, up to thirty years of age . . . " still appear in Japanese newspapers.

To some extent, Japanese women may sometimes be naive accomplices to their being shut out of Japanese corporate life. In a book written in 1981, a successful woman advertising entrepreneur, Yuriko Saisho, advised would-be Japanese women managers to utilize their native trait of *nikkori*, which means "with a smile." Ms. Saisho's quaint advice:

> [*Nikkori*] is the greatest charm women possess. A woman's smile softens the atmosphere. In an all-male meeting, when a woman is added, even though she may not say anything, just her presence and her smile [will be beneficial]. A woman's smile is closely related to the warmth and all-encompassing understanding of Mother Earth, and this mollifies the minds of men.[1]

As if to highlight their lower status, Japanese spoken by women is simply not the same language as Japanese spoken by men. The grammatical structures employed by women, especially when they are speaking to men, designate an almost feudal subservience. Women must almost unfailingly use superpolite vocabulary and verb forms. It is hard to imagine how a Japanese female manager can ever succeed in giving a direct order to a male. It will be interesting to observe possible linguistic changes if and when Japanese women become managers in significant numbers.

In the face of such apparently unabated Japanese male chauvinism

---

[1] Yuriko Saisho, Women Executives in Japan (Tokyo: Yuri International, 1981), p. 64.

and linguistic bias, can an American woman reasonably hope to do business with the Japanese either in Japan or in the United States? The answer is not clear cut. There is a certain percentage of Japanese businessmen who are simply incapable of conducting serious business with a woman.[2] However, other mitigating factors and their own persistence have made it possible for some American women, including Caucasians, African Americans, and Asian Americans, to succeed in overcoming Japanese sexism, not to mention racism and ethnocentrism discussed shortly.

... first impressions have an especially powerful effect on the Japanese. The reward for making a favorable first impression on Japanese businessmen is limitless admiration and loyalty.

First, while Asian-American women may have a greater familiarity with the thinking patterns of "the enemy," Caucasian and African American women may have an advantage over Asian-American women in one respect. A lack of subservience is probably less startling to a traditional Japanese male when displayed by a woman who does not look Japanese. He may be more open-minded about the role of a woman who already is unfamiliar looking. For the same reason, an American woman doing business with Japanese males is well advised not to do anything that plays into the traditional Japanese businessman's expectations regarding the role of women. When a Japanese visits an American woman's office, she should avoid pouring coffee or extending other courtesies that might be misinterpreted as stereotypical Japanese female obsequiousness. If it can be arranged, it is best for a young male to serve coffee at the specific request of the American woman. This gesture will communicate that it is the woman who is in charge of the situation. It is also worthwhile briefing male colleagues and making sure that they take every opportunity to express their confidence in their female colleague and unlimited respect for her professional judgment.

It is best if a woman's entire manner of dress and demeanor are as gender neutral as possible. When she meets a particular Japanese businessman for the first time, the barely feminized suits and ties popular in

---

[2]Undoubtedly, there is also a certain, probably much smaller percentage of American businessmen who share the same outlook.

the 1970s, when women first joined corporate America in more than negligible numbers, are probably best. Chanel suits should be reserved until after the relationship is well established.

While the foregoing admonitions may seem trivial, first impressions have an especially powerful effect on the Japanese. The reward for making a favorable first impression on Japanese businessmen is limitless admiration and loyalty.

Ironically, because Japanese lack experience in dealing with professional women, a foreign woman is particularly well situated to mold their initial experience and win them over.

To illustrate, about a decade ago, a group of Japanese managers from a large electronics company arrived at their Honolulu hotel for the first meeting with their New York lawyer who would be assisting them in a tough negotiation the next day with an American company. They were dumbstruck when their American lawyer turned out to be a woman. While the Japanese party was standing at the registration desk in varying degrees of discomfort, the clerk told the lawyer that the hotel did not have her reservation and that it was fully booked that night. She was firm and insistent that the clerk rectify the situation to her satisfaction immediately, which he did. The Japanese turned from dumbstruck to awestruck and decided that any mere female who could stand up to the clerk and get her way would be a formidable advocate for their company. The Japanese company has remained her loyal client.

RACISM

Japanese do not regard themselves as racist. However, in the authors' estimation, Japanese are capable of displaying extremely provincial, naive attitudes toward non-Asians and non-Japanese Asians, which by any American standard must be counted as racist.

Japanese may be susceptible to racism because of two central characteristics of Japanese society: homogeneity and vertical structure. The former makes the Japanese peculiarly unsophisticated in their understanding of outsiders; the latter makes it difficult for them to relate to others as equals. No matter how marginal the difference in station between two or more individuals, Japanese are compelled to calculate who is inferior and who is superior.

Throughout most of history, the average Japanese has had few contacts with foreigners, fewer contacts with Caucasians, and even fewer with African-Americans. Perhaps as a result of this inexperience, Japanese attitudes toward African-Americans can be shockingly naive. A view that presumably educated Japanese apparently do not hesitate to air publicly is that African-Americans excel in sports and entertainment, but are incapable of coping with intellectual endeavors. As recently as 1987, former Prime Minister Nakasone stated publicly that the problem of low American academic achievement is a result of the country's large number of Blacks and Puerto Ricans. As recently as 1989, a Japanese toy company marketed a Black Sambo doll.

No matter how marginal the difference in station between two or more individuals, Japanese are compelled to calculate who is inferior and who is superior.

Japanese naivete is not confined to African-Americans. Caucasians are sometimes stereotyped as being stingy, aggressive, disloyal, and cruel to old people. In addition, many Japanese lack understanding of the differences among Caucasian ethnic or religious groups. However, lack of understanding does not seem to impede mainstream Japanese publishers from producing anti-Semitic books that seem to sell well.

Some Japanese also take a negative view of other Asians, which is reflected in the way products from other Asian countries are marketed. For example, although trade between Japan and Korea flourishes, Korean products are sometimes marketed in Japan under different names, and vice versa.

Koreans and Chinese understandably return Japanese antipathy. Asians do not readily intermarry, either between themselves or with members of other races. A Japanese magazine was recently quoted to the effect that for Crown Prince Naruhito to marry a foreigner is "as unthinkable as Godzilla being elected President of the United States."[3] One must wonder if the writer meant to imply that as between Godzilla and a foreigner, Godzilla, being of Japanese origin, would be preferred as a match for the prince.

How to deal with Japanese racism? First, it should be noted that Japanese racism and ethnocentricism are almost never manifest in one-on-one rudeness. Because Japanese racist attitudes are generally based on the lack of contact with outsiders, such attitudes tend not to be well entrenched and crumble quickly in the face of experience. Japanese who

---

[3]*The Chicago Tribune*, February 10, 1991, p. 21.

spend any length of time in the United States learn to admire American aspirations of racial equality and justice and are embarrassed by their less experienced countrymen.

To summarize,

1. It is probably a waste of time to send an emissary to Japan under the age of 40 to open a relationship with a Japanese company.

2. Women, non-Asians, and even other Asians may still encounter obstacles in Japan based on gender, race, and ethnicity. However, such obstacles can be overcome.

3. When dealing with Japanese males, businesswomen should refrain from performing service tasks associated with a traditional role and should take every opportunity to demonstrate professional leadership.

PART II
MAKING
CONNECTIONS

Part II addresses issues you may face in initiating contacts with Japanese businesspeople. First, it is important to know how Japanese organizations are structured in order to be aware of exactly whom you are making contact with, what power they do or do not exercise within their own organization, and how decisions are made. Second, it is important to know how to approach Japanese business organizations through a suitable individual or corporate "go-between," as well as what to expect at a first meeting. The final chapter of Part II is devoted to the surprisingly important function of and protocol regarding Japanese business cards.

6 Japanese Business Organizations

To communicate effectively with the Japanese business world, it is first necessary to gain an understanding of the fundamental differences between Japanese and American business organizations. Those differences are largely a reflection of the way in which virtually all of Japanese society is organized.

More than 20 years ago, in a book that has become a classic description of Japanese society, Professor Chie Nakane observed a defining difference between Japanese and Western social organizations.[1] Although Ms. Nakane's observations were not geared specifically toward business organizations, her analysis provides an extremely useful framework for explaining how decisions are made in Japanese companies, how promotion and compensation are structured, why Japan has certain labor practices, and how communication takes place both intra- and inter-organizationally.

Japanese companies can best be described as "vertical." In vertical organizations, membership is a function of what Ms. Nakane calls "frame." Frame may be a locality, an institution, or a particular relationship that binds a set of individuals into a single group. Unlike Japanese business organizations, American business organizations are "horizontal." The members of the group are not bound by frame, but are selected because of certain attributes. Attributes are particular skills or know-how

---

[1]Chie Nakane, *Japanese Society* (Berkeley and Los Angeles: University of California Press, 1970). A professor of cultural anthropology, Ms. Nakane was the first woman to reach the rank of full professor at Tokyo University, which has the status in Japan of all the Ivy League schools and Stanford rolled into one.

that serve the organization's current needs. When the organization no longer requires an individual's particular attribute, the individual becomes obsolete. There is no longer any recognized basis for the individual's membership in the group. In an American company (horizontal), an employee whose attribute is the ability to design car doors understands that he will be let go if the company goes out of the car-making business.

In a Japanese company, however, the basis for membership is not attribute, but frame. An employee's identification with the organization is total. His attributes may change, but they are immaterial as a basis for membership in the organization. If he has acquired the ability to design car doors and the company goes out of the business of making cars and into the business of making rocket engines, the company will train him to design rocket engines. If it would be unrealistic to train him to design rocket engines, perhaps he could be trained as a maintenance engineer in the plant.

Foreigners have often made the correct observation that Japanese companies function like families. This is not surprising; the family is the prototype vertical group. One does not become a member of a family because of attributes. Membership in a family is based on an assumption of belonging forever. A baby is born into a family as the embodiment of potential. As it grows, it learns skills that fulfill the family's needs; for example, a child takes out the garbage, a teenager with a driver's license does errands, an adult child contributes financially, and so on. The adults in the family care for the young and the young are supposed to obey the adults. Certainly it is assumed that one of the goals of the family is the welfare of its members.

Japanese companies function much the same as families. College graduates enter the company immediately upon graduation from college, not for their attributes, but for their potential. As they continue to work for the company they will not be differentiated by attribute, but by rank. Their world will be divided into three groups: *sempai*, or seniors, *kohai*, or juniors, and *dohai*, or equals. The first group includes everyone who was in the company before him. The second consists of everyone who joined the company after him. And the third is limited only to those who came to the company as part of the same class of graduates.

There is very little lateral hiring and really nothing like the detailed job descriptions typical in American companies. Under such circumstances, someone who does join the company mid-career is at a disadvantage. Although the system may be changing to some extent, anyone who comes into a Japanese company starts at the bottom of the totem pole.

Interestingly, as a general rule Japanese students approach their college studies rather more casually than do American college students.

This is because their Japanese employers are indifferent to the graduates' specific skills; it is assumed that anyone who has managed to pass the stunningly rigorous entrance examination to a top Japanese university has already demonstrated brains and perseverance. From a Japanese company's point of view, specific skills will be learned as needed. Since the graduate is joining up for life, there is no hesitation to expend company resources on training him. It is quite common, even for a graduate with a technical degree, to be rotated through various of the company's departments for several years. Of course, many American companies also have rotation policies; however, Japanese companies tend to rotate employees rather more widely and for a greater length of time. It is also quite common for Japanese companies to sponsor promising employees who have been in the organization for several years for sometimes lengthy graduate studies abroad if there is some know-how that the company lacks.

... the Japanese wage system is designed so that compensation is adequate to meet the expected needs of an employee at each stage of his life.

By contrast, an American college student intent on securing lucrative employment is best served by acquiring specific, saleable skills. An American employer does not buy a person, but an engineer, an accountant, a computer specialist, and so on. The newly minted liberal arts B.A. is often the least attractive as an employee from an American employer's perspective. An American student is expected to acquire skills at his or her own cost in graduate school, not at the expense of a company with which the duration of employment is anybody's guess.

Japanese compensation and promotion practices also reflect the vertical nature of Japanese companies. Since members are not thought of as being differentiated by attributes but by seniority, promotions are lock step. Raises in compensation also generally move lock step. The focus on seniority over merit exists through the rank of *kacho*, or section chief, which in a large company is usually achieved when the employee reaches his mid-forties. Since obviously not everybody can become president, a vice president, or even a division head, after this point, merit prevails and seniority is no longer the overriding factor in determining compensation. Those employees who are not destined to advance beyond *kacho* are sometimes known as *mannen kacho*, or "ten-thousand year section chiefs."

Lack of advancement, however, does not signify financial hardship. Because a vertical organization inevitably has as one of its goals the welfare of its members, the Japanese wage system is designed so that compensation is adequate to meet the expected needs of an employee at each stage of his life.

Accordingly, the ratio between an employee's beginning salary and his top salary is much greater in Japan than in the United States As an example, in Japan, a public school teacher's top salary is at least five times greater than his starting salary. In the United States, it is only three times as much. In some Japanese companies, even employees who do not reach upper managerial ranks may earn seven times as much at their peak salary as they did when they started.

Starting salaries are relatively low. New college graduates are likely to be single, live in subsidized company dormitories, and do much of their socializing at the company's expense. However, a Japanese graduate knows from the day he joins the company that when the time comes, he will be paid enough money to send his children to college and to meet his social obligations. Until recently, he also used to be sure that he would be able to buy a house at least by retirement age. However, in view of the stratospheric land prices in urban areas, buying a house has become impossible for any average Japanese whose income is limited to a salary and interest on savings.

It should not be surprising that when Americans accustomed to operating in horizontal American organizations are hired to work in vertical Japanese companies, whether placed at the home office in Tokyo or at the American subsidiary in New York, friction is not infrequent. Japanese bosses may resent younger American employees with highly marketable professional or technical skills who often must be paid higher salaries than the bosses'. If American employees are asked, as they often are, by their Japanese bosses to perform a task outside their official job description, they may feel entitled to refuse. In the horizontal organizations to which they are accustomed, American employees do not feel particularly responsible for the success and welfare of the entire organization; they are satisfied that they have done everything they should if they have properly carried out the tasks related to the attributes for which they were hired.

The fact that most Japanese business organizations are vertical complicates their ability to undertake joint ventures successfully, whether among themselves or with foreign companies. The very nature of joint ventures mandates horizontal organization. Joint venture companies are established to fulfill specific purposes that can often be accomplished in a relatively short span of time. They are certainly not organized to benefit their employees. Persons with specific attributes needed by the joint venture are selected from each organization. Everyone is selected to fulfill a discrete job description that clearly defines the borders of their responsibilities. In such an organization, many Japanese employees feel that they have been placed in an inhospitable environment.

In a vertically organized company, employees identify more with the company itself that with their own individual attributes. Thus, they do not readily feel limitations on the scope of their responsibilities. In such a setting it is just as likely that ideas for change emerge from among the lower ranks of employees as from the boardroom. Japanese companies are known for their "quality circles" and other formal and informal mechanisms that allow ideas to filter up through the ranks.

Informal communication among employees is encouraged and facilitated partly by the physical layout of offices. Japanese corporate offices are generally laid out in a big room. Only the very highest-ranking executives are separated from the group, and even then, the separation may consist of nothing more than plate glass. The selection of physical environment is deliberate. Japanese call it *obeyashugi*, or "big roomism." This is in contrast to the physical arrangement of American corporations where employees strive for a private office with an outside window. Interestingly, under the *obeyashugi* system, persons seated near the windows are likely to be *mannen kacho*. Employees lacking capability who have reached a rank solely by virtue of seniority are sometimes called "window people" (*mado no hito*) because they are given little to do and are said to spend most of the day looking out of the window.

The informal communication that takes place among peers and with their immediate supervisors is known as *nemawashi*. At this juncture, ideas tend not to be put in writing. Their merits and drawbacks are discussed at what may seem to Americans to be a leisurely pace. Finally, when an idea has been thoroughly massaged through the *nemawashi* process and consensus seems likely, it is committed to writing in a document called a *ringisho*, which is simply the official memorialization of a plan or strategy after the completion of *nemawashi*. The *ringisho* is circulated among key members in the company who will have responsibility for implementation of the plan or strategy and anyone whose approval of it is required. If an employee has no objection to the contents of the *ringisho*, he will affix his *hanko*, or individual seal, to the *ringisho*. If there are objections, additional *nemawashi* will ensue in order that a consensus can be reached. Only when all the *hanko* have been acquired will the final decision to go ahead be made.

As American lawyers who have prosecuted product liability claims against Japanese corporations will confirm, under this consensus system, it is virtually impossible to fix blame for a bad decision on a few individuals. The Japanese system of fixing blame does not require such identification. In situations where someone must take the blame for disastrous results, responsibility resides with the entire group or at the top. Thus, when a Japan Air Lines 747 went down killing hundreds, even though the cause had absolutely no connection to his specific actions, the president of Japan Air Lines resigned. We personally know of a situation in which the chief engineer of a showcase bridge construction project resigned after his chauffeur was involved in an after-hours drunk driving accident that resulted in a death.

This system, of course, contrasts with the typical mechanisms of American corporate decision making. In an American company, a vice president of research and development may come up with an idea for a new product. He may then leave his office to share the idea, usually with someone who is at least at his level within the company. A major decision may be reached by a handful of high-ranking executives, sometimes within a matter of days. At this stage, employees with the hands-on responsibility of implementing the decision may or may not have been included in the loop of communication.

Style of leadership in a vertical business organization is somewhat different from what American business leaders are used to. As a Japanese executive climbs to the upper reaches of the corporate ladder, he is not likely to be familiar with the company's operational details or even to have a perfect understanding of the latest technological developments in his industry. Instead, Japanese executives are more likely to have reached the top by displaying superb interpersonal skills.

Charisma, in the Western sense, is not a quality possessed by most traditional Japanese corporate leaders. Instead, they tend to adopt a *teishisei* or "low-posture style." They cultivate slow, deliberate speech and behave with outward humility, subscribing to the Japanese saying that "the ripest rice stalk bows its head the lowest" (*minoreba, minoru hodo atama no sagaru, inahokana*). Japanese leaders do not feel that admitting mistakes reflects weakness and may begin many statements with a pro forma apology.[2]

Of course, others within the Japanese organization know better than to misinterpret their leader's humble demeanor as lack of power. Sometimes, Americans do not know better. Used to the dynamic, even aggressive style of American leaders such as Iacocca, Trump, or the late Armand

---

[2]There are a few, well-known Japanese corporate leaders who do not fit the traditional mold. For example, Mr. Morita of Sony, Mr. Honda of Honda, and Mr. Inamori of Kyocera, while no longer young, are still "upstarts" known for their outspokeness. Mr. Morita is a sought-after speaker the world around.

Hammer,[3] they often misdirect their attention to the wrong person in a Japanese organization, or they almost unconsciously, and at their peril, ignore the most important Japanese person at the meeting.

Before leaving the discussion of Japanese business organization, a final point should be made: The universality in Japan of vertical organizations and the all encompassing demands that such organizations make upon their members may be diminishing to some extent. The Japanese press today is filled with stories about what many Japanese perceive are the harmful effects of unbridled devotion to the company, for example, the brutal working hours, the effect on younger employees of emphasizing seniority over merit, friendships being largely limited to business associates, and the like. In the last decade there have been previously unheard-of defections from Japanese corporate life: Expatriates choose to remain abroad and start their own businesses; even senior Japanese executives have bolted and joined American or European companies. It will certainly be interesting to observe whether any deep, widespread changes evolve in Japanese business culture or whether those who abandon the system remain a newsworthy handful.

To summarize,

1. Japanese corporations can best be described as "vertical." They function like families and offer their members secure employment.

2. Specific skills are not the basis for membership in Japanese companies.

3. Decisions in Japanese companies are made by consensus.

4. Mistakes are the responsibility of the entire group. Often the leader of an organization takes full responsibility for the actions of subordinates.

5. Japanese corporate leaders are known more for their interpersonal skills than for charisma.

---

[3]Of course, dynamism in Western leaders in neither limited to Americans, nor to business. Western heads of state during World War II—Churchill, De Gaulle, Roosevelt, Mussolini, and Hitler—were all talented orators having strong, distinctive personalities. By contrast, Tojo was anything but charismatic. He could barely manage a public speech. This lack of charisma was not a deterrent to leading, or misleading, the nation.

7 Opening Doors

American businesspeople who have tried to make contacts with Japanese companies in the same way that they approach domestic companies will not succeed. Japanese view a face-to-face contact, initiated by a credible intermediary, as virtually the only acceptable way to begin a serious business relationship.

Anywhere in the world, there are three basic channels through which businesspeople make their first contacts with customers, suppliers, potential partners, financiers, or any others in whom they have a business-related interest. The first is the cold call. The second is to write a letter introducing yourself and enclosing materials relevant to the purpose of the contact, and the third is to be introduced by an intermediary. The third means can occur informally at a social or quasi-social occasion, such as a business association meeting or a formal party. It can also be arranged from the start as a business meeting.

In the American business world, all three methods of making a first contact are considered to have inherent utility. Of course, one method may be considered more efficient or likely to succeed in a given situation than another. It is not at all implausible that even a high-ranking executive would personally pick up the telephone to contact a prospective supplier whom he has never met and may not know very much about. Nor would it be considered unusual for the executive to call someone with whom he is not personally acquainted to invite that person out to lunch if he believes that they have something of mutual business interest to discuss. Making cold telephone calls to potential customers is, of course, a standard marketing tool in a wide spectrum of consumer service industries. In the

United States, method two is often the method of choice for first contacting potential customers for business services, as well as for consumer services.

Neither method one nor method two works in Japan except in very limited circumstances that apply primarily to consumers, the main exception being door-to-door sales. Items sold door to door in Japan go far beyond the typical household goods that are the stock in trade of Fuller Brush or Amway. Even automobiles are sold door to door during hard times. Retail investment brokerage is also carried out door to door as contrasted to American-style telemarketing. As described in *The House of Nomura* by Albert J. Alletzhauer,[1] a securities broker's harrowing initiation to sales is often a stint as a door-to-door salesman in a Japanese backwater. Similarly, chieftains of the largest banks in Japan today recall that their first assignment after joining the bank was the door-to-door solicitation of new savings accounts.

Nevertheless, the cold call as an attempted means of establishing business-to-business contact is considered insolent and aggressive. If a Japanese executive wishes to establish contact with a person he does not know or with another organization, he must enlist the services of a *shokainin* or *shokaisha*, that is, someone who acts in the capacity of official introducer. A business, often a trading company (*sogo shosha*), or a bank can function in the same capacity.

The role of *shokainin* is both broader and more responsible than that of an American intermediary. First, the *shokainin* literally vouches for the parties he is introducing. His responsibility is not extinguished after the parties' first meeting, but may continue for the duration of their relationship. If the relationship between the parties is successful, he will receive part of the credit and the unending gratitude of both parties. Similarly, the blame will fall partly on his head if one or the other of the parties defaults or in some other fashion does not behave properly in the relationship. If something goes wrong or if there is a dispute between the parties, the *shokainin* may be pressed back into service to straighten things out. Thus, a potential *shokainin* will not necessarily agree to an engagement simply because he happens to know both parties.

One of the authors had the unpleasant experience of "losing face" by agreeing too readily to serve in the capacity of *shokainin* for an acquaintance who is the CEO of a *Fortune* 500 company. Despite being carefully briefed, the CEO, used to doing things his own way, breached Japanese business etiquette at every turn, appearing aggressive and thankless in Japanese eyes. As a result, the authors' own credibility with those

---

[1] Albert J. Alletzhauer, *The House of Nomura* (New York, Arcade, 1990).

to whom the CEO had been introduced was squandered. It took an apology and explanation to restore the status quo.

Being asked to serve as a *shokainin* is considered an honor and an acknowledgment of the *shokainin's* wisdom, experience, and reputation. For the individual *shokainin*, no specific monetary remuneration is generally either discussed or expected. However, if the contact arranged by the *shokainin* results in establishing a business relationship, a gift that reflects the importance of the new relationship is in order.[2]

Of course, it is not always easy to find a *shokainin*. If the introduction sought has the potential to result in a significant transaction, Japanese companies may spend months locating the best possible person willing to serve. Naturally, the more stature possessed by the *shokainin*, the better. Emeritus executives or high-level former bureaucrats regularly serve as *shokainin*. Executives will contact the company's bankers or executives they know within the same enterprise group[3] to try to uncover the right *shokainin*. They may even consult their college's alumni directory since school connections are considered important, lifelong, and a credible basis for maintaining old relationships and forming new ones. Japanese alumni associations thrive around the world.

Increasingly, with the internationalization of business, foreigners serve quasi-*shokainin*. A British banker may find himself in the role of intermediary between, say, a Japanese and an American client. As a general rule, most Japanese businesspeople accept bankers as *shokainin* more readily than lawyers. In Japan, the only lawyers officially designated as such who are members of the bar (*bengoshi*) are really the equivalent of English barristers or American litigators. Since they are generally encountered in an adversarial environment, Japanese do not view lawyers as being the best *shokainin*. Of course, Japanese who have spent time in the United States and have become acquainted with American corporate lawyers understand that they can be very useful as *shokainin*.

If the quest for an individual *shokainin* fails, institutional *shokainin* will have to suffice. One organization that functions in this capacity is JETRO, the Japan External Trade Organization. The original mission of JETRO when it was founded after Word War II was to promote Japanese

---

[2]The traditional matchmaker in Japan, the nakodo, works under a similar arrangement, but expects monetary remuneration in accordance with an unpublished, but well-known, going rate if a marriage ensues. The payment is referred to not as compensation, but as orei which simply means "thanks."

[3]The well-known Japanese enterprise groups, or *keiretsu*, are groups of companies with significant cross-ownership. Although the number and nature of the companies may vary from one *keiretsu* to another, most *keiretsu* consist of one or more manufacturers, a bank, a trading company, a wholesaler, and perhaps an insurance company.

exports. Today, JETRO's mission has undergone a 180-degree turn. JETRO now tries to assist those who seek to export products and services to Japan.

Officially, JETRO does not operate as an agent of any particular government ministry. However, its key staff members who are responsible for policy decisions are generally on loan from another ministry, often the Ministry of International Trade and Industry (MITI). These powerful borrowed staff members are known as *shukko*. Sometimes JETRO also houses personnel who come from other ministries or represent particular cities, regions of the country, or industries.

Like a traditional *shokainin*, JETRO does not serve casually. A potential user of JETRO's services as an intermediary must first establish his own credibility. Matters can be expedited if a company can locate a *shokainin* who can introduce its executives or board members to the right person at JETRO.

Another organization that has proved useful to Americans who wish to develop Japanese business connections is the Japanese Chamber of Commerce and Industry located in most major American cities. The Japanese Chamber is an increasingly powerful organization. The Chicago branch currently boasts over 400 corporate members. Virtually every Japanese-owned business in the area is a member. Occasionally, membership is extended to non-Japanese-owned businesses or to Americans who are not of Japanese ancestry.

Within the last decade, another type of organization has begun to play an important role in providing a setting for Japanese and American businesspeople to establish connections. Begun even before World War II as small groups whose interests were centered on Japanese art and culture, the Japan-America societies are now at least as much, if not more, focused on business and topics of particular interest to businesspeople. The societies flourish in most major cities. For example, the Japan-America Society of Chicago currently has some 2,000 members, many of whom are key representatives of Japanese and United States companies. Most meetings address bilateral trade issues, Japanese politics, the workings of particular Japanese industries, and the like. The meetings provide fertile ground for networking and locating potential *shokainin*.

Finally, *sogo shosha*, the giant Japanese general trading companies having worldwide operations, will serve as commercial *shokainin* for agreed-upon remuneration. It is said that for a Japanese trading company to qualify as a genuine *sogo shosha*, it must be capable of handling everything from noodles to satellites. A *sogo shosha's* capabilities include consulting, financing, locating property, and assisting in procuring any applicable licenses, just to mention a few. In some cases, a *sogo shosha* will actually take an interest, sometimes a significant one, in the enterprise it represents or in a joint venture founded with its assistance.

Japanese attach a great significance to first meetings.

Despite a Japanese preference for establishing contacts through the conventional means described so far, unconventional means occasionally succeed where need overwhelms custom. For example, some years ago, a well-known Japanese automaker decided to establish a manufacturing facility in the United States Since under the Japanese system, it either would not or could not hire away executives with appropriate experience from other automakers, it sent a group of its own managers, completely inexperienced in doing business in the United States, on what must have seemed to them a "mission impossible" to set up the facility. Under the circumstances, tradition was ignored and the hapless group welcomed the approach of any American organization interested in helping them locate real estate, housing, insurance, or providing information that could be of assistance to them, *shokainin* or no. In such a situation, a cold call could do no harm; in fact, at least one American business that contacted the Japanese group by cold calling was rewarded with a lucrative contract. The lesson is that it is always worthwhile to be alert and on the lookout for the odd situation where desperate people scrap convention.

Once a *shokainin* is located and has arranged a first meeting, an important phase ends and a new phase begins in the process of establishing business relationships. The *shokainin* may or may not be present at the first meeting. If he does not attend, he will have sent in advance or will provide you with a letter of introduction and/or his *meishi* with a brief note about you written on it. If he does attend the first meeting, he may or may not leave before the meeting is concluded. Japanese attach a great significance to first meetings.

Whether an important first meeting takes place in Japan or elsewhere, it is a virtual certainty that the Japanese will have gone to great lengths to learn everything they can, both about the organization and the individuals who will be representing the organization at the meeting. Investigation that goes beyond publicly available information is not unusual if the prospective relationship is thought to have significant potential. Inquiries may even have been made about the education, work history, as well as the families and personal interests of the individuals involved.

First meetings with Japanese are akin to opening ceremonies. If the first meeting physically takes place in a Japanese office, from an American point of view, it may seem formal to the point of being ritualistic. Nothing is left to chance. From the time that the business visitor arrives at the door and is appropriately greeted to the time that he is seen off from the sidewalk in front of the office building as his car or taxi pulls away, attention will have been given to every detail, including seating arrangement and refreshments and, perhaps even to what artwork is to be hung in the meeting room that day.

Insofar as is practicable, some of the same formality and attention should be injected into a first meeting that takes place at American offices. Ideally, American staff members who come in contact with a Japanese visitor should be briefed as to Japanese names (Chapter Nine), bowing (Chapter Thirteen), the use of business cards (Chapter Eight), seating arrangements (Chapter Fifteen), and dress code (Chapter Thirteen). Those who will participate substantively in any meeting should not only be more extensively briefed, that is, have an acquaintance with the topics in this book, but should be prepared to demonstrate that they have taken the time and made the effort to know as much about their Japanese visitors as the visitors know about them. This does not always come naturally because Americans generally consider the scope of information relevant to making a business decision narrower than do the Japanese.

For much the same reason, Americans should not necessarily expect that at a first meeting, Japanese will willingly discuss what Americans view as "business." This is especially true in a first meeting that includes high-level executives. The Japanese are apt to be inclined to discuss, politely and apparently casually, everything from sports and world events to topics that Americans consider plainly private, for example, marital status, number and ages of children and where they attend school, interests and hobbies. It is not that Americans do not also enjoy chatting before commencing substantive business discussion, but their attention span is limited to 5 or 10 minutes, after which they want to "get on with it." On the other hand, Japanese believe that they *are* getting on with it, "it" being the mutual establishment of personal credentials, in the absence of which they are extremely reluctant to progress to the next stage of commitment. In other words, what Americans view as collateral to doing business, Japanese view as falling squarely within the business agenda. It may take one, two, or even more meetings before discussion turns to a potential transaction; however, the American businessperson capable of resisting the temptation to insist on "getting down to business" and allowing the Japanese to take the lead in this regard may be rewarded by a long-term relationship far less vulnerable to the vicissitudes of price and market conditions than he is used to.[4]

To summarize,

1. It is worth taking the time to find a suitable *shokainin*, but stay alert for situations where Japanese might consider establishing a relationship without a *shokainin*.

2. Knowledge of Japanese business etiquette is an essential part of your preparation for a first meeting.

3. Japanese will insist on getting to know you and will have learned a great deal about you and your company before you get there.

---

[4]Nothing in the last two paragraphs should be confused with garden-variety stalling that may take place *after* personal credentials are established and the parties are in the thick of negotiations.

8 Handling *Meishi*

Japanese customs associated with the use of businesss cards have become fairly well known to many American businesspeople. Nevertheless, the way that Japanese regard and use business cards bears repeating.

The Japanese word for business cards is *meishi*. Physically, of course, business cards and *meishi* are virtually identical. They are about the same size and impart roughly the same information, although the *meishi* may well have more information regarding job title. However, the respective protocols for their use are vastly different, partly, as will be seen, because of what is by American standards the rigidly hierarchical nature of Japanese society.

To an American, a business card functions simply as a practical reminder of a person's business affiliation and of how that person may be reached should the need arise. As such, it is treated rather casually. Business cards are usually exchanged at the end of a meeting, or upon actual leave taking, with little attention or ceremony. Nor is it out of the range of acceptable business protocol for someone not to happen to be carrying a business card. A piece of paper can serve as a substitute if addresses or telephone numbers need to be exchanged.

For Japanese businesspeople, however, *meishi* are indispensable. The 12 million *meishi* exchanged daily amount to a staggering 4.4 billion annually.[1] The information on the *meishi* informs innumerable aspects of the subsequent interaction between the people who exchange them. This is so because the identity of their respective business organizations combined with the respective positions they hold in those organizations

---

[1] *Business Tokyo Magazine,* October 1987.

determines their rank relative to one another. A rather more detailed description of position than that appearing on an American business card may facilitate the process of mutual evaluation. It would not be unusual for the Japanese job title to be something as detailed as "Deputy Section Chief Dealing With Plastic Products." Unfortunately, the job description translated into English is not always as detailed.

Only after two or more Japanese have completed a silent calculus and determined their relative status do they know how deeply to bow, and what form of address and grammatical inflections to use in order to speak with the appropriate level of politeness or familiarity. Without knowledge of respective rank, communication may be strained and tentative.

Care should be taken to translate designations of rank in a way that permits Japanese to interpret rank correctly. Because certain American business organizations have platoons of vice presidents, it can be misleading for the title to be used on a business card translated into Japanese. Even an American vice president who is in charge of a division or a major department would be referred to in Japanese as *bucho*, which literally means "division head," and not as *fukushacho*, which means "vice president," in the sense of true second in command.

Japanese exchange *meishi at the very beginning* of the first meeting, virtually before they exchange their first words. Since only in the privacy of his home can a Japanese businessperson divest himself of his role as such, he carries his *meishi* with him everywhere. He is almost as likely to be called upon to produce it at a golf course, a bar or restaurant, or in an airplane as at the office. The *meishi* can even serve as an identification card. This is true whether in Japan or abroad. Even we have accepted the necessity of carrying *meishi* when we shop at a Japanese grocery store in a suburb of Chicago.

Meishi are handled with care. They are kept in a quality holder and in pristine condition. Although there may be a certain slackening of standards especially among Japanese in the United States, *meishi* should be delivered face up with both hands. Their presentation should be accompanied by an appropriate bow. *Meishi* should not be carried in a hip pocket. Nor should a *meishi* received from another person be placed there. Following presentation, each person takes one or two moments to read, or at least to pretend to read, the other's *meishi*. Since the presentation of the *meishi* is essentially the presentation of the self, putting away another person's *meishi* without at least giving the appearance of reading it is decidedly rude.

For similar reasons of showing respect, traditional Japanese do not use someone else's *meishi* as a substitute for a memo pad, at least not in their presence. However, someone else's *meishi* may be used as an informal letter of introduction, in which case it will be presented by the person being introduced together with his own *meishi*. For example, Mr. Suzuki may provide his colleague Mr. Honda with a *meishi* with a note on it to present to Mr. Brown, with whom Mr. Suzuki is acquainted. The note is likely to say something such as "Please take good care of my colleague Mr. Honda."

Meishi must also be exchanged in group situations. The people in the host or ranking group present their *meishi* first, from the highest ranking to lowest ranking, in order. The process may take some time, but it is one that is considered essential. If a meeting takes place at a table, the participants typically place the *meishi* of others in a configuration that reflects where everyone is seated. Not only is doing so acceptable, it is quite expected and very convenient. Even in a meeting having numerous participants, each person knows exactly who is speaking and who is being addressed.

Virtually no Japanese businessperson would consider traveling abroad without a bilingual business card or separate English and Japanese business cards. Yet, even today, Americans bound for Japan often do not bother to have bilingual business cards prepared. There are two reasons why it is strongly recommended that Americans use bilingual business cards in Japan. The first is an obvious, practical one, and the second is more subtle.

Many American names are *very* difficult for Japanese to pronounce because they contain certain sounds such as those represented by "f," "l," "r," and "th" that simply do not exist in Japanese and/or that Japanese cannot readily distinguish from other sounds. Many Japanese have a hard time hearing these sounds, let alone reproducing them. "Fitzgerald" and "Rosenthal" are two of many examples of reasonably common "American" names that are overwhelmingly difficult for most Japanese. Unless they are recast in some form manageable for Japanese speakers, these names are certainly unlikely to be remembered. On a bilingual business card, they will be transcribed in Japanese phonetic symbols known as *katakana*. Correctly transcribed in *katakana*, these names will be pronounced by Japanese as "Fittsugerarudo" and "Rozensaaru"—but at least they *will* be pronounced and, more important, perhaps remembered.

Sometimes Americans leave the transcription into *katakana* of their names, as well as their company's name, up to the printer. However, it should be apparent that bilingual business cards must be prepared by someone who not only understands rank within both Japanese and American business organizations, but is also well schooled in the phonetics of both English and Japanese. There are many bilingual business cards in circulation that sport Western names needlessly butchered beyond recognition. The transcription of many Western names has in the last 5 to 10 years become relatively standardized. A bilingual business card prepared by someone unfamiliar with an existing standardized form of transcription has the potential to be embarrassing. Of course, the preparer's services should include proofreading the business cards once they are "camera ready." Also, the same competent preparer should be used for business cards of all personnel in order to ensure uniformity in the transcription of the company's name as well as uniformity in the designation of rank.

The second reason to prepare bilingual business cards is psychological. When American economic hegemony was unchallenged, Japanese did not expect to see bilingual business cards. Many Japanese who still serve in decision-making positions remember the sense of being part of just another small, developing nation. Today, they feel second to none and expect to be met at least half-way by foreigners with whom they do business. A bilingual business card can serve as much appreciated evidence that you understand their sensibilities.

One final suggestion: Remember if you are traveling to more than one Asian country to prepare separate bilingual business cards for each. Americans on occasion have presented bilingual English-Japanese business cards to Koreans or Chinese without ever realizing the offensiveness of the gesture. Not surprisingly, many Asians continue to resent Japanese and do not applaud Japan's resurgence and entry into the international community. While Americans may focus on similarities among Asians, Asians are more likely to focus on their important differences.

To summarize,

1. You will exchange business cards at the very beginning of your first meeting with a Japanese.

2. You should present your business card with two hands, printed side up.

3. You will want to keep your business card in a quality holder.

4. It is important that you look at the other person's *meishi* before you put it away.

5. Bilingual business cards should be prepared by someone who has a thorough knowledge of Japanese and American business organizations as well as of Japanese and English phonetics. Have the same person prepare the bilingual business cards of everyone in your organization.

6. *Meishi* are carried at all times.

7. Three to five times the number of *meishi* you think necessary should be carried if you are bound for Japan. In an emergency, most Tokyo hotels that cater to foreigners can help you obtain bilingual *meishi* relatively quickly.

8. *Meishi* should not be carried in your hip pocket.

PART III
VERBAL
COMMUNICATION

Part III addresses assorted issues regarding communication through the medium of words. Japanese names and forms of address are explained in Chapter Nine. Chapter Ten deals with what might be termed Japanese "verbal rituals," culturally encoded forms of expression that are easily misinterpreted by Westerners. Finally, Chapter Eleven treats the subject of how to speak through interpreters.

9 The Rules of Names

The form one selects to address another person serves to establish the appropriate level of formality based on such considerations as the nature of the relationship, the setting, and the presence or absence of other people. Using the wrong form of address can result in giving genuine offense.

In American English, a change in form of address often signals a change, or at least a desired change, in the relationship with the person addressed. However, the basic rule of thumb in Japan is that the form of address used in the first meeting between the parties is good for life—and after—regardless of how close a business relationship or friendship becomes. Despite any disparity that develops in social milieu, status, or title, the relative status between the parties remains the same. For example, a Japanese prime minister was visited by his former elementary school teacher whom he had not seen for decades. The prime minister greeted the retired teacher with a deep, formal bow and added the customary honorific to the teacher's name (*sensei*). The teacher, on the other hand, addressed the prime minister with the same casualness and using the same form of address, *Sato-kun*, as he did in the days when the prime minister was playing in the schoolyard. It is as though Mr. Justice Holmes were to be addressed as "Ollie" by an elementary school classmate whom he had not seen since eighth grade. In other words, no matter how much time has elapsed and no matter how lofty the professional ascent of one person relative to the other, the form and manner of address remain the same.

When Americans meet for the first time, in business as well as social situations, even when they are introduced by an honorific followed by a family name, for example, "Dr. Smith," they are impelled to move as quickly as possible to a "first name basis." This shift, which depending on the situation can take from 5 minutes to 5 years, is supposed to demonstrate the shedding of pretense and the beginning of a relationship of trust: "Call me 'Bill.'"

In many circumstances, the failure of the shift to occur may signal that the relationship is going nowhere. For example, if at the end of a series of interviews for a professional position, the person being interviewed is still being addressed as "Ms. Jones" instead of "Mary," Ms. Mary Jones unfortunately might be correct in surmising that she failed to win the interest of the prospective employer.

Of course, in American business culture, the switch to first names may express an aspiration of trust rather than its achievement. A salesperson, for example, may begin calling a potential customer by his first name even if there is little possibility of ever seeing the customer again. In other business situations as well, Americans believe that it is good marketing to express the aspiration of trust at an early stage.

By contrast, Japanese—as well as Chinese, Koreans, and most other Asians, do not equate trust, honesty, or closeness with being on a first name basis. Nor is there any "progression" from last name to first name that reflects a parallel progression in the quality of the relationship. Simply stated, in Japan there is absolutely no equivalent of "getting on a first name basis." For an F.O.B., being called by his given name by someone he met for the first time as an adult would be an alarming experience.

In fact, few Japanese have a genuine understanding of what Americans mean by "being on a first name basis." For example, when he was president, Ronald Reagan and former Japanese Premier Yasuhiro Nakasone developed what the American press dubbed the "Ron-Yasu" relationship. Such a description of the cordiality that developed between these two powerful men simply would not make sense to most Japanese. Even those Japanese cabinet minister closest to Nakasone would never refer to him as Yasuhiro, let alone Yasu.

Even Japanese who are familiar with American customs may feel very uncomfortable being addressed by their first names except by those with whom they have close family or school relationships, and then only when the family member or schoolmate is of an equal or higher rank. However, occasionally, an S.O.B. will proffer an invitation to be called by his first name or an abbreviation of his first name that is easy for Americans to pronounce. For example, Mr. Yoshitsune Saito may suggest, "just call me Yoshi." He may even ask to be called by an adopted Christian first name so that American friends will not be burdened by the task of trying to remember a Japanese name. Of course, such an invitation should be graciously accepted with one important proviso: If other Japanese are present, Mr. Saito may become embarrassed and regret his invitation. For the same reason, in any letter written to him at his company in Japan—which is likely to be seen by others—it is wiser to write "Dear Mr. Saito."

Like Westerners, Japanese have family names and given names. They never have middle names. An exception to the rule may occur when a Japanese has become a Christian and assumes a baptismal name, or when he intentionally Westernizes his name to comply with the practice of using a middle name.

If a person's full name is stated in Japanese, the family name goes first followed by the given name. In a Japanese-English bilingual *meishi*, the side in English follows English name order, given name followed by family name, and the Japanese side follows Japanese name order.[1]

The generic form of address for both adult men and women (defined as anyone who has completed formal schooling) is "san." For example, an adult whose family name is Suzuki and given name is Hiroshi would be addressed as "Suzuki Hiroshi-san" or "Suzuki-san."

Sama is another form of address used for adult men and women that denotes an extremely high level of respect. Accordingly, it is frequently used when addressing clients or customers, particularly in very formal or impersonal situations. For example, the word for "honorable guest" is *okyaku*. Professional greeters stationed at the entrance to department stores in Japan will address customers as *oyaku-sama*. *Sama* is also generally used on public address systems.

Very small children, both boys and girls, are generally addressed by their given name followed by *chan*, which signifies the diminutive form. A girl will continue to be addressed as *chan* while, outside the family, a boy will begin to be addressed as *kun* once he reaches school age. A girl in the third grade whose given name is *Mariko* will be addressed by family members, friends, and teachers as simply *Mariko-chan*. A boy whose given name is *Masao* will be addressed as *Masao-chan* by his family and *Masao-kun* by schoolmates and teachers. Once *Mariko* and *Masao* reach high school, *Mariko's* teachers will address her by her family name followed by *san* and *Masao* will be addressed by his family name followed by *kun*. Family name plus *kun* is also used by adult males within the same organization, but only from higher to lower ranking, or among peers.

Japanese often address and refer to others, particularly their superiors, by (1) rank or professional designation alone–*kacho* [section chief]

---

[1]This is not always true in the case of English-Chinese or English-Korean name cards where the rules of name order are not stringently applied. The given name is generally followed by one of several forms of address.

—or (2) rank or professional designation following family name–*Saito-kacho*–or (3) rank followed by *san* or *sama–kacho-san*.

Another often heard professional designation is *sensei*. It is applied to all doctors and all teachers in whatever level of school. In addition, lawyers, diplomats, and politicians, and anyone who has been recognized as having reached the highest level of achievement in his profession, should also be addressed as *sensei*. For example, the well-known senior Japanese actor, Toshiro Mifune, is addressed as *Mifune-sensei*. Like other forms of address that designate profession or rank, *sensei* can stand alone or follow a family name. However, *sensei* is never followed by *san* or *sama*.

To summarize,

1. It is always safe to address an adult Japanese using family name followed by *san*.

2. You should address a very small child by his or her first name followed by *chan*. Address an older child by his or her first name followed by *san*.

3. Form of address is not a barometer of success or failure. Do not anticipate any change in form of address and do not suggest one.

4. You should never use anybody's first name unless you are invited to do so. Revert to family name when others are present.

5. When speaking in English, it is acceptable to say "Mr. Tanaka" or "Ms. Saito;" however, "Mr. Tanaka-san" or "Ms. Saito-san" are incorrect and sound silly.

6. *Kun* cannot be used by outsiders.

10 Verbal Rituals

WHY MISINTERPRETATION OCCURS

In every linguistic culture there evolve distinct characteristics and patterns of expression, usually traceable to prevailing cultural norms. A New Orleans taxi driver may say, "Begging your pardon, Ma'am?" In the same situation a New York taxi driver who speaks the "same" language is much more apt to say, "Pardon?" or simply "What?" The difference in the "form" of the taxi drivers' statements is neither fortuitous nor inconsequential. A passenger from New Orleans who is unfamiliar with the culture of New York City is apt to misinterpret the New York taxi driver's statement as reflecting antipathy. On the other hand, a passenger from New York City is likely to misinterpret the statement of the New Orleans taxi driver as conveying a special regard for her personally. However, the message that both taxi drivers intended to convey is probably identical: "I did not hear what you said." Both taxi drivers structured their statements in a form that would be correctly understood by natives of their own cities or others who understand the respective cultures of those cities, but made the statements susceptible to misinterpretation by untutored outsiders.

We choose to call distinctive, culture-based forms of expression "verbal rituals." Without an understanding of Japanese verbal rituals, it is all too easy for Americans to miss entirely the true meaning of statements Japanese make.

Before discussing particular Japanese verbal rituals and contrasting them to typical American verbal rituals, it should be pointed out that just as in the United States, verbal rituals may vary from region to region within Japan. For example, a common greeting among Osaka merchants is *Mokarimakka*, which means "Are you making any money?" The greeting, unbelievably crude by Tokyo standards, does not require a literal response. The intent of the Osaka speaker is really no different from that of the Tokyoite proffering the standard *ikaga desu ka*, translated as "How are things going?" However, general differences between American and Japanese verbal rituals are far greater than regional differences within either country.

VERBAL RITUALS REGARDING ONESELF AND ONE'S COMPANY

Japanese and American verbal rituals regarding expressions of self are acutely different. American cultural values of independence and autonomy are demonstrated in Americans' typically unself-conscious reference to their actual or perceived abilities. An American asked whether he plays tennis may respond, "Oh, yes, I play quite a bit," meaning "Whenever the weather is good and I have a free hour, I try to get to the courts." By contrast, a Japanese who values interdependence, harmony, and face is more likely to respond, "I suppose I play a little tennis," even when the reality is that he is an amateur champion capable of blowing nine out of ten recreational tennis players off the courts. If these two ever play tennis together, the American will think that the Japanese was "sandbagging," and the Japanese will think that the American was at best bragging and at worst lying. In short, when Japanese say they are "acquainted" with a theory, a process, a technology, or whatever, it is safe to assume that, by American standards, they are discounting the actual state of their capability or knowledge.

Japanese also tend publicly to discount the worthiness of subordinates. A parent my ask a teacher or other caretaker of a cherished child to "please take care of my worthless son."

Just as Japanese will try to belittle themselves and any subordinate in their "family," including their company, to outsiders, they publicly exalt the accomplishments of others. Any visitor to Japan who manages to say two words in Japanese will be told his Japanese is excellent and praised for his linguistic talent. This type of praise should not be accepted at face value.

The same contrast in verbal ritual applies when the topic is one's company. The contrast is especially acute at first meetings, which Americans often view as an opportunity to say as much about their business as they can possibly squeeze in during the time allotted. They tend to tout their company's accomplishments and minimize its failings. They may even use the occasion to denigrate competitors.

Apart from the fact that such an approach entirely misses the purpose of a first meeting as the Japanese see it, the style is all wrong. Of course, Japanese businesspeople try to make other businesspeople aware of their company's merits, but it is accomplished only in due course and with subtlety. Making disparaging remarks about competitors is considered very bad form, especially before a close relationship has been cemented. Even then, while communicating in the *tatemae* mode, competitors are almost never criticized.

The marked difference in Japanese and American verbal rituals when referring to one's company have been observed by the authors on numerous occasions. In a particularly memorable incident, one of us brought an American colleague with special expertise in an area of interest to Japanese banks to a luncheon where top representatives of many Japanese banks were sure to be present. Obviously some parts of the pre-luncheon briefing given to the colleague stuck better than others. After an impeccably executed bow and exchange of *meishi* with the very well-connected and powerful Japanese banker next to whom he was seated, the young American launched into a nonstop litany of his professional achievements that lasted for the duration of the lunch. He did not notice the banker's relief when the after-lunch speaker took the podium. The American thought that the interruption in the "conversation" caused by the speaker was the main obstacle in an otherwise golden opportunity to secure business from the bank. He simply did not realize that he had already lost it 5 minutes into the meal.

We also vividly recall a contrasting experience. An effective and successful underwriter from one of the largest Japanese securities houses was invited to make a presentation to a representative of an American corporation with a view toward persuading the American company to list its shares on the Tokyo Stock Exchange. In typical Japanese fashion, the underwriter made a careful, low-key presentation, emphasizing both the costs and potential disadvantages of listing as well and the potential benefits. He got no points for his candor, no recognition of his status or the status of his company, and no farther than the initial presentation. Not long thereafter, the American company did list its shares on the Tokyo Stock Exchange, but struck the deal, perhaps at a higher price, with an American securities underwriter acting as an intermediary. In other words, the company did not end up dealing directly with the Japanese in this instance.

THE ROLE OF APOLOGY

The American emphasis on independence as contrasted to the Japanese reliance on interdependence is evident in the respective use of apology, or the lack thereof, in the two business cultures. In general, Americans do not readily apologize, even when a mistake has clearly been made. An apology for someone else's mistake as though it were one's own and without mentioning the involvement of the other person is even rarer. And an unqualified apology may be the rarest of all. In Japanese business culture, where indulgence is freely sought and expected in exchange for obedience and humility, apologies are made at the drop of a hat.

To Americans, Japanese seem to apologize for everything from inconsequential mistakes to the weather or the negligible pace of Tokyo traffic. Significant mistakes engender not only an apology by the person directly responsible for the mistake, often hard to identify anyway, but also by the entire group and/or its leader.

In Japanese business culture, where indulgence is freely sought and expected in exchange for obedience and humility, apologies are made at the drop of a hat.

It should be understood that apology in the Japanese context is not necessarily a painful experience accompanied by feelings of guilt if the situation causes no particular loss of face. For example, a Japanese apologizing for the unworthiness of a gift is not really expressing a feeling of guilt for having shopped carelessly, but is performing a ritual for seeking indulgence. It makes no sense in this context to join an excuse or explanation to the apology. When Americans equivocate or shift blame onto others in the same breath that they utter the apology, Japanese find the apology insincere. While we are not suggesting that Americans adopt the Japanese practice of apologizing at every turn, we do suggest that apologies to Japanese be stated freely and unequivocally.

YES, NO, AND MAYBE

There are at least four Japanese words that are translated into English as "yes." They are *hah*, *hai*, *eh*, and *un* in descending level of formality. The most formal of the group is *hah*. It carries the connotation of "I will obey." Today its use is limited to the world of Japanese organized crime (*yakuza*) and to situations where someone, such as a hotel clerk or waiter, is responding to a patron's specific request.

Hai is the standard, polite form of yes, *eh* is somewhat less formal, and *un* is reserved for family members and for close, usually male, peers. Less than half of the time do any of these forms of "yes" mean "Yes, you're right" or "Yes, that's correct." In the majority of cases, the speaker means "I'm listening" or "Go on." A subordinate is apt to inject a *hai* after many of his superior's statements, whether or not the statements embody a directive or request. Imbued with the Japanese sense of the word *hai*, Japanese speaking in English sometimes mislead Americans because they say "yes" when they mean to say something like "I understand" or "uh huh."

It is well known and has been noted in Chapter Two that Japanese find it difficult to make and state a clear personal judgment when presented with a choice. Of course, they have no trouble making definite statements regarding external phenomena in which no one's "face" is involved. For example, if presented with a question such as "Has it started raining?" Japanese have no more difficulty saying "yes" or "no" than do Americans. However, when their own face or the face of another person is at stake, Japanese believe it is kinder, and even more truthful, given the mutable nature of reality, to equivocate. Thus, "yes" is often followed by the word "but" left hanging in the air as in the phrase, "*Eh, demo.*"

Japanese also avoid the unequivocal "no" embodied in the Japanese word *iie*, which is heard infrequently except to deny praise given by another. Even in the example "Has it started raining?" a less direct and, therefore, more polite negative answer such as *chigaimasu*, meaning "the truth is different," is preferred. From the Japanese point of view, such an answer does not obfuscate, but shows consideration for the other's face. That is not to say that the Japanese are less capable of subterfuge and dissembling than are Americans. It is simply that the Japanese tendency to refrain from definite yes's and no's is usually grounded on other considerations.

Japanese have many ways of saying no while avoiding a harsh and potentially face-destroying *iie*. The Japanese have long been aware that their view of the appropriate use of "yes" and "no" is different from that of Americans and other Westerners. In 1972, Keiko Ueda, then a student at Tokyo's International Christian University, wrote a senior thesis titled "The Japanese Pattern of Declining Requests," in which she identified 16 verbal rituals that Japanese use to express that they will not be fulfilling a given request.[1] Ms. Ueda's observations, based on interviews with Japanese mothers who were asked how they would say no to a request to serve on a PTA committee, were reproduced as "Sixteen Ways to Say No in Japan." The verbal rituals identified are not only clearly understandable by Japanese, but are applicable in business settings as well as in the particular setting explored by Ms. Ueda.

Japanese may say "no" by insisting that someone else is more capable of successfully executing a project. They may tell a white lie that usually involves some personal rather than business contingency such as "we can't take a meeting this week because the daughter of one of our directors is ill." They may say they cannot respond immediately or that they must review the situation further.

Another favorite way to say "no" that is often misunderstood as a "yes" by Americans is *Zensho shimasu* which translates "we'll try our best." Prime Minister Kakuei Tanaka visited Richard Nixon at the White House and was pressed by Nixon to increase Japanese expenditures on defense beyond 1 percent of Japan's GNP. Even before Tanaka left Japan, he knew that it would be politically impossible for him to do so. When the question came up in the talks, Tanaka replied *"Zensho shimasu."* Nixon reported to the American press that this time he had succeeded in persuading the Japanese to increase their defense budget. Japanese present at the talks knew differently. Americans should understand that when Japanese talk about "doing their best," they mean that they want to maintain goodwill in case something can be done later. However, nothing is going to happen immediately.

To summarize,

1. Discounting Japanese expressions of modesty and expressions of praise by 50–75 percent is recommended.

2. Criticism of competitors is frowned on. Any criticism should be made only when the *honne* mode is in use and should be scrupulously accurate.

3. Generous apologies are appreciated; take full responsibility for the mistakes of subordinates, but do not shift any blame to them or others.

4. The use of *hai*, or less formal forms of "yes" do not necessarily indicate agreement.

5. There are many verbal rituals that Japanese use in lieu of "no" that Americans are apt to misinterpret as meaning "yes" or "maybe."

---

[1]Ms. Ueda's article is printed in J. C. Condon and M. Saito, eds., *Intercultural Encounters in Japan* (Tokyo: Simul Press, 1974) pp. 185–192. The list is reprinted in John L. Graham and Yoshihiro Sano's *Smart Bargaining* (Cambridge, Mass.: Ballinger, 1984), p. 24.

11 The Use and Misuse of Interpreters

Most Americans instinctively dislike the idea of communicating through an interpreter. Americans tend to view interpreters as interlopers who interfere with "direct" communication. This sentiment comports with the American preference for a "do-it-yourself" approach. However, learning to be comfortable speaking through an interpreter and knowing how to use an interpreter effectively can spell the difference between the success or failure of your mission.

SIMULTANEOUS VERSUS CONSECUTIVE TRANSLATION

Simultaneous translation occurs when an interpreter renders a translation at the same time that the speaker speaks. This is the type of translation that typically takes place in public forums, such as when a speaker addresses the United Nations. In consecutive translation the speaker stops speaking after one or more sentences and waits while the interpreter translates what the speaker has finished saying. Only when the interpreter completes the translation does the speaker resume speaking.

Very few interpreters are capable of doing simultaneous translation between English and Japanese. Those who are charge premium rates beginning at $500 per day. However, the lavish expense of simultaneous translation should not discourage the use of interpreters because simultaneous translation is neither necessary nor desirable under most circumstances.

At first blush it would seem that apart from the extra expense, simultaneous translation is always preferable. Negotiations that are conducted through simultaneous translation would appear to require only half the time of negotiations conducted using consecutive translation. Moreover, it would seem that since an interpreter capable of simultaneous translation would almost by definition be more skilled , the quality of the translation is likely to be better.

Upon closer scrutiny, these presumptions fail. First, rarely is time so much of the essence that accuracy can be sacrificed. Second, no matter how skilled the interpreter who translates simultaneously, the interpreter who translates consecutively has so many patent advantages that the disparity in skills would have to be overwhelming for the simultaneous translation to be more accurate than the consecutive translation.

Profound differences between English and Japanese sentence structure are responsible for making simultaneous translation between English and Japanese particularly difficult. In English, the essential elements of a sentence are generally rendered in the first few words. The action of the sentence, the main verb, is usually immediately preceded by the identification of the actor and immediately followed by the object of the action. The opposite is the case in Japanese. The main elements of a sentence are rendered at the end. The result is that it is virtually impossible for an interpreter to begin to translate an English sentence into Japanese until the entire English sentence is completed because the elements that are likely to go at the end of the English sentence are likely to go at the beginning of the Japanese sentence. The interpreter is required to listen to the entire English sentence before uttering a single word, remember the sentence as a unit, and speak the entire sentence in Japanese—while at the same time memorizing the next spoken English sentence as a unit in order to be able to render it in Japanese! By contrast, an interpreter translating simultaneously from English to, say, French, which has a sentence structure much closer to English, can usually begin rendering a French translation of an English speaker's sentence almost as soon as the first word is uttered.

To illustrate: Consider the English sentence

"I saw Mr. Jones in December of 1949."

The main verb, "saw" appears early in the sentence immediately preceded by the actor "I" and immediately followed by the object of the action, "Mr. Jones." The same sentence as structured in Japanese becomes

"[I][1] 1949's December in, Mr. Jones saw."

(*Watashiwa 1949-nen' no 12-gatsu ni Joonzu-san ni aimashita.*)

---

[1] In nine out of ten Japanese sentences, the subject is omitted because it is understood from context.

To take a slightly more complex sentence,

"The lawyer suspected that the company could not get the financing to complete the acquisition."

The same sentence structured in Japanese becomes

"The lawyer the company acquisition complete to the financing could not get suspected."

(*Sono bengoshi wa sono kaisha ga baishuu o surutameno yuushi o ukerarenaidaroo to omotteita.*)

The interpreter cannot begin to render the English sentence into Japanese until the English speaker has completed it. For the simple sentence in the example, an agile interpreter may be able to keep up, provided that the sentence is followed by equally simple sentences. However, the waiting, memorizing, and rendering of the entire English sentence into Japanese while listening to the next sentence in English can overwhelm even the most skilled interpreters. Inevitably, parts of some English sentences simply get skipped—unless the speaker knows ahead of time more or less what the speaker is going to say.

A more straightforward memorization problem can occur even for the interpreter translating consecutively if the speaker pauses only after paragraphs instead of after one or two sentences. The speaker inadvertently overburdens interpreter's capacity for memorization. The lesson is that when you are speaking through an interpreter, the best translation results when you discipline yourself to pause for the translation at very short intervals.

Even the best interpreter occasionally does not know the meaning of an English word, in which case the word either gets misinterpreted or omitted. A consecutive translator is far more likely to be able to discern the meaning of a word from context because the interpreter can listen in "units" without having to worry about rendering the translation at the same instant that the speaker is speaking.

Finally, the slowing down of a negotiation by the use of interpreters translating consecutively offers a benefit in addition to more accurate translation. During the time that the interpreter is speaking, the negotiator's attention can be fully focused on any nonverbal reactions of the other party. While an experienced negotiator presumably will either mask—or deliberately choreograph—a reaction to the other party's statement, there is often something to be learned by carefully observing the other party's unintentional body language. Thus, the time during which the interpreter is speaking can often be put to excellent use. In fact, some experienced negotiators find this aspect of consecutive translation so beneficial that they will choose to speak through an interpreter even when they are perfectly capable of speaking in the listener's language.[2]

JOKES, JARGON, JAPANESE WORDS, ADAGES, NUMBERS

(1) Jokes

Jokes rarely translate. Humor is one of the most culturally rooted forms of communication. This accounts for the existence of anthologies of ethnic humor. No matter how universal you think that your joke may be, do not use it unless you have discussed it thoroughly *in advance* with an interpreter whom you know and trust to be candid with you if the joke is inappropriate or is simply not amenable to translation. Sometimes the interpreter can even suggest an alternative joke that will convey the same substance.

Similarly, hyperbole does not translate into Japanese. A Japanese will take the statement, "I could kill him" literally and will assume the speaker is capable of and actually intends to carry out a murder. Even typical English expressions such as "I love it" or "I hate it" don't play well—or at least don't play accurately—in Tokyo. The Japanese listener will assume an intensity of emotion that the speaker probably does not intend. Moreover, the Japanese listener is likely to be embarrassed, if not appalled, that the speaker would share such an intense, personal emotion with anyone other than a spouse or best friend.

(2) Jargon

Be cautious in using jargon. If possible, consult in advance with your interpreter to determine if the jargon you may use is known to the interpreter and is likely to be known to your Japanese audience. For example, a particular Japanese listener or group of listeners may not be aware of such expressions as "voice mail," "poison pill," "virtual reality," "golden parachute," or "rainmaker." On the other hand, if you are quite sure that your particular audience is sufficiently internationalized to be familiar with these expressions, they may be flattered by your confidence in their understanding as reflected by your use of such expressions.

---

[2]Edwin O. Reischauer, consistently used interpreters. A former U.S. ambassador to Japan, Mr. Reischauer was born and raised by missionary parents in Japan and married a Japanese. His Japanese was so good that he was seen from time to time correcting his interpreters, but chose not to speak Japanese on most official occasions.

(3) Japanese Words

Do not assume that English words of Japanese origin mean the same thing in Japanese. For example, "honcho" (*hancho*) in English means the person in charge. The term connotes a truly powerful individual. However, the same word in Japanese means something closer to "squad leader" and connotes a functionary capable of carrying out someone else's policy. The president of Honda Motors would certainly be insulted by being referred to as a *hancho*.

Another Japanese phrase that many Americans picked up watching the television miniseries *Shogun* is consistently misused. Endlessly uttered in the course of the TV series was *wakarimasuka*, which means "do you understand." Judged solely by its literal meaning, it would seem to be a good phrase to know. However, no right-minded Japanese businessperson would ever say it to another. The phrase is laden with condescension and is an expression of doubt that the other person has the ability to understand. If you must ask if someone has understood something, the appropriate expression is the superpolite *owakari desuka*. It should be noted that although *wakarimasuka* is grammatically a "polite" construction of the verb *wakaru*, when uttered to a superior, it is unmistakably impolite. When uttered to a co-equal or subordinate, it is merely brusque.

Another category of "Japanese" that Westerners occasionally use to their detriment consists of corruptions of Japanese words coined by American G.I.s stationed in Japan. An example is *daijobi*, an American corruption of the Japanese word *dai joo bu*, which means roughly the equivalent of "O.K." Use of such words is definitely *declassé*.

(4) Adages

As a general proposition, in the United States a person's level of education and sophistication is often measured by the ability to communicate "original" thoughts. In Japan, these same qualities tend to be measured by a person's mastery of numerous adages and sayings often derived from classical literature, both Oriental and Western. If you want to impress a Japanese, it cannot hurt to make a few maxims of ancient Oriental wisdom part of your vocabulary. However, be cautioned that some American sayings will be incomprehensible and embarrassing to your interpreter, not to mention your Japanese listeners. Even sayings that are literally identical in both Japanese and English do not always mean the same thing.

Examples of the former are "priming the pump" and "flying by the seat of one's pants." An example of the latter is the adage, "a rolling stone gathers no moss," (*tenseki koke musazu*), which is literally identical in Japanese and English. However, Japanese uniformly understand this phrase to mean that "a person who pursues a single project tenaciously will succeed." The message is that it is best to "stay put." By contrast, a group of American executives who were recently asked what the phrase meant uniformly interpreted it as reflecting the principle that "to get ahead, it is important to keep moving."[3] The lesson here, as always, is to consult in advance with your interpreter.

(5) Big Numbers

When your negotiations involve numbers of 100,000 or more be sure to write out the numbers for your interpreter. Japanese count by units of 10,000. Thus 10,000 is stated in Japanese as one ten-thousand, or one *man*. 100,000 is stated in Japanese as ten ten-thousands (*juu man*), and 1 million is stated in Japanese as one hundred ten-thousands (*hyaku man*). The greater the number, the greater the potential for confusion. At an exchange rate of, say 130 yen to the dollar, the numbers can get very large indeed. Even seasoned international businesspeople who are very familiar with the differences in the respective American and Japanese ways of rendering numbers are confused from time to time, if only momentarily. The solution is to write down numbers for your interpreter.

HIRING YOUR OWN INTERPRETER

It is strongly recommended that you engage and pay for your own interpreter even if the other party has already hired an interpreter. Ideally, it might seem that good interpreters should be interchangeable machines that produce identical translations of the same material. Reality is far from this supposed ideal. Moreover, even the most "accurate" translation machine is incapable of capturing nuance, or reading between the lines to arrive at a clearer understanding of the speaker's intended meaning. A joke that circulates among professional interpreters illustrates the point. Someone invented a perfect translation machine. The machine's first assignment was to translate "Out of sight, out of mind" from English into a Hindi dialect. The machine promptly produced a faithful translation: "invisible idiot."

Because human communication is never mechanistic, the benefit of mutual briefing between interpreter and client—as well as debriefing—cannot be overemphasized. It goes without saying that you cannot

---

[3]The adage is actually of British origin. Most British interpret it the way Japanese do, perhaps because in both Britain and Japan, there is a tradition of cultivating moss in formal gardens. It is understood that moss will not grow on a stone that is moved about.

brief and debrief an interpreter whom the other party has hired and paid for.

The best interpreters are products of a liberal arts education who have read widely rather than of an education in a technical field. However, legal terms, financial terms, medical terms, and any other terms peculiar to a particular discipline or industry often stump these interpreters if they encounter them for the first time in the course of interpreting them. You will do both yourself and your interpreter a favor if you provide your interpreter with a vocabulary list of words common in your field well in advance of an engagement and provide the opportunity for your interpreter to ask you questions about your list.

Finally, take advantage of a debriefing session to ensure that your understanding of the other party's position concurs with the interpreter's understanding. Even though the interpreter may have rendered a literally accurate translation, the other party's real meaning may partially depend upon cultural norms that are simply incapable of being conveyed in literal translation. As discussed, American listeners hear "we'll do our best" as meaning that there is at least a 50 percent probability that a goal will be met. To the Japanese, "we'll do our best" (*zensho shimasu*) is generally a euphemism for "at present, we can do nothing," especially if the word "but" (*kedo* or *keredomo*) is left hanging at the end of the phrase.

What an interpreter can tell you in the course of a debriefing is sometimes more illuminating than what was translated during the actual negotiation. In short, a good interpreter is better than a machine.

To summarize,

1. Interpreters should be used liberally; the benefit of a good interpreter always outweighs cost.
2. A simultaneous translator should be used *only* when a written text of what the speaker is going to say can be made available beforehand; consecutive translation is almost always preferable for negotiations.
3. Jargon should be used with caution or avoided altogether.
4. Use of hyperbole is not appropriate.
5. Words of Japanese origin that have worked their way into English should be avoided.
6. It is advisable to write down all numbers that exceed 100,000.
7. Jokes or adages should not be used unless you have discussed them previously with your interpreter.
8. You should not rely on another party's interpreter; always hire

your own interpreter no matter how redundant doing so may seem.

9. As far as possible in advance of a negotiation, you should provide your interpreter with a vocabulary list of words peculiar to your industry.

10. A debriefing by your interpreter is an obvious benefit.

PART IV
NONVERBAL
COMMUNICATION

People tend to think of "communication" in the narrow sense: written or spoken words, manifest as what is audible or visible in print. However, no matter where we are or what we are doing, as long as there are other people who can see us, hear us, or touch us, we are transmitting and receiving messages through virtually limitless forms of non-verbal communication. Nonverbal communication includes posture, gait, gestures, eye contact, the use of silence, and the like. Nonverbal signals often are more telling of what is actually meant to be communicated than are the accompanying words.

Verbal communications are not always perfectly clear. However, if there is doubt that an intended meaning was actually conveyed, words can be repeated or explained using other words. Generally, either the maker or the recipient of the communication can initiate the process of clarification. By contrast, nonverbal communications are fraught with a peculiar peril: They can neither be taken back nor explained. Moreover, the potentially disastrous results of misinterpretation may not become known until months or years later.

Nonverbal communications are no less culture bound than are languages, food preferences, or kinship systems. An understanding of what Japanese convey nonverbally is sure to enhance successful communication with Japanese businesspeople.

12 Distances, Eye Contact, Silence

PROXEMICS

Proxemics is a term coined in the 1970s by Northwestern University anthropology professor Edward Hall. It signifies the distance people keep between themselves in various social situations. People operating within the same culture know, without giving the matter any thought, how far apart to stand during a first meeting, whether it is appropriate to shake hands or hug, or how close to stand at a cocktail reception. Moving closer than the situation calls for will be interpreted, depending upon the specific circumstances, either as aggressive, presuming an unwarranted degree of friendship, or as a sexual advance. Placing oneself too far away from another person in a given situation will be interpreted as standoffishness, a lack of interest, or even enmity or disgust.

The Japanese person places himself at a distance that is uncomfortably far for the American.

As a general rule, given the same circumstances, Japanese tend to keep a greater physical distance than Americans. A result of this discrepancy can sometimes be observed when a Japanese and American are conversing in a hotel lobby or at a reception. The Japanese person places himself at a distance that is uncomfortably far for the American. The American responds by unconsciously inching toward the Japanese. The Japanese responds to the American's advance by moving slightly backward. The ensuing minuet can be quite amusing.

Except in the crowds of Tokyo where it is virtually impossible, adult Japanese ordinarily avoid physical contact. The social hug or kiss on the cheek is nonexistent. Even parents do not hug their adult children. Other types of physical contact more or less typical in the West as indications of friendliness are equally foreign to Japanese. For example, lightly tapping a conversation partner on the arm, if done by a man to a woman or a woman to a man, has the potential to be misinterpreted by the Japanese as a sexual advance. Back slapping, a not uncommon gesture of goodwill among American businessmen, will be perceived by most Japanese as extremely low class. Even Japanese who have lived in the United States and are well acquainted with Western customs will often be made extremely uncomfortable by physical contact.

By contrast, certain types of physical contact between members of the same sex frequently seen in Japan may be repugnant to or misunderstood by Americans. For example, there is no connotation of homosexuality between high school or college boys who walk together arm on shoulder, or between girls of the same age who walk together holding hands.

EYE CONTACT

In most respects Japanese and Americans have squarely opposing views of what constitutes appropriate eye contact. As a result, the opportunity for mutual misunderstanding is great. With particular exceptions, Japanese traditionally are trained not to maintain eye contact. As a result, Americans sometimes report what they perceive as Japanese impoliteness, lack of attention, or shyness. Traditionally, the only person in a Japanese group who can look straight into other peoples' eyes is the oldest or highest-ranking male. All others avert their eyes by looking down, closing their eyes, or shifting focus, depending upon the circumstances. Japanese college graduates seeking their first jobs are admonished by career counselors to look just below the interviewer's tie knot.

A breach of eye contact etiquette by looking at another person squarely in the eye may be considered too aggressive. Japanese gangsters known as *yakuza* speak of looking someone in the eye as *gan o kiru* or "cutting his face." The gesture is considered purposefully threatening and can provoke retaliation.

By contrast, Americans equate "shifty eyes" with dishonesty. In his book *Plain Speaking*,[1] Harry Truman described Richard Nixon as a "shifty-eyed goddam liar." Expressing a similar American sentiment regarding eye contact is the admonition in a training manual for flight attendants used by a large U.S, airline that opened U.S.–Japan routes several years ago: Be sure to maintain eye contact when speaking with passengers. However, this is poor advice for flight attendants dealing with Japanese passengers. Middle-aged Japanese males would be very likely to misinterpret deliberate eye contact from a female—especially a younger female—as insolence or as being sexually suggestive.

In the same vein, when an American parent doubts the truth of a child's statement, the parent is apt to respond by demanding, "Look me in the eye and tell me (what time you got home last night, or whom you were out with, etc.)" The American adolescent is expected to look the speaker in the eye during a scolding. A Japanese adolescent who failed to keep eyes averted in the same situation would be viewed as asking for additional punishment.

SILENCE

Although the maxim that "silence is golden" is well known in both the United States and Japan, in reality Americans and Japanese have demonstrably different attitudes towards silence. They do not experience silence during discourse in the same way. For Americans, silence in business or social settings is almost always negative. Five seconds of silence at an American dinner party creates an uncomfortable void that the diners, and especially the host or hostess, will feel compelled to fill. In a business setting, silence in response to a proposal is considered either negative or indicative of the other party's failure to understand the proposal. The person whose proposal is greeted with silence is likely after only a few seconds to say, "Well, what do you think?" or "Do you have any questions?"

Unlike Americans, Japanese view silence, at least in the absence of other signals, as basically neutral. Silence may reflect a wide range of emotions from sadness or anger on the negative side to serenity, pleasure, or satisfaction on the positive.

For example, it is not uncommon for Americans who entertain Japanese at dinner for the first time to think that something has gone terribly wrong because the conversation "ball" did not keep rolling. The Americans worry that the silences that abounded during the evening

---

[1] Harry Truman, *Plain Speaking*

indicate that they somehow may have given offense to their Japanese guests. The Americans are totally surprised when their Japanese guests offer them profuse thanks at the end of the evening, mention the "wonderful" occasion many times at future meetings, send an expensive gift, or reciprocate with unparalleled hospitality in Japan.

Somewhat similarly, silence during a business meeting or negotiation may mean nothing more than that the Japanese listener has taken what was said seriously enough to consider it carefully. The very hesitation that makes Americans uncomfortable signifies nothing more than the Japanese listener's respectfulness, or his need for more time to consider. The Japanese negotiator feels no compulsion to keep talking while thinking.

American misapprehension of typical Japanese silences can be costly. The example destined to become a classic was reported in the August 1, 1983, issue of *Time* Magazine, which was devoted entirely to Japan. ITT and a major Japanese firm had for some time been negotiating a large contract. To consummate the deal, ITT brass went to Tokyo to meet their Japanese counterparts. The head of the Japanese company was asked to sign the contract just presented; he lapsed into silence. The Americans quickly sweetened the deal by $250,000. An observer at the meeting, the late Howard Van Zandt, business professor at the University of Texas, claimed that the Japanese silence was totally misinterpreted by the Americans. ITT took a quarter of a million dollar hit that could have been avoided by a modest cultural briefing.

The Japanese negotiator feels no compulsion to keep talking while thinking.

The degree to which an individual Japanese is silent or talkative during a business meeting may have implications regarding rank. The highest-ranking Japanese is often the quietest at the meeting. An important caveat: The *lowest* ranking is also likely to remain silent. However, some other obvious factor, such as youthfulness, will be a giveaway. On the occasions when the number one person does speak, his speech is likely to be slow, brief, ponderous, even perhaps pompous by American standards. Japanese top persons may be striving for *kanroku*, a term that defies translation but roughly it means "quiet weightiness." The *kanroku* "style" befits *haragei*.

Speaking is generally the province of the middle manager who is likely to be the most voluble and eager, and often the best English speaker.

As a result, Americans sometimes fall into the trap of addressing themselves during a meeting to a relatively lower-ranking person. The result may be an inadvertent slighting of the Japanese who has the real decision-making power.

To summarize,

1. Japanese generally keep a greater physical distance between themselves and others than do Americans.

2. Adult Japanese do not engage in casual, social physical contact with other adults.

3. In Japan, only the highest-ranking male is allowed to look directly into another person's eyes.

4. Any attempt by someone other than the highest-ranking male to make direct eye-contact is apt to be interpreted as purposeful aggression.

5. There is no reason to be concerned or intimidated if a Japanese remains silent; for Japanese, silence is neutral and can signify feelings ranging from satisfaction to sorrow or anger. Avoid the impulse to break a silence quickly.

6. The highest-ranking member among a group of Japanese businesspeople is likely to be the most silent.

7. The person who knows English best and is the most voluble is unlikely to be the leader of the group.

13 How to Show Who You Are

DRESS CODE

Why talk about dress code in a book about communication? Because, as in many other things, Japanese do not discriminate between form and substance.

Westerners may tend to view the Japanese attitude as an exultation of form over substance. A more accurate characterization, however, is probably that for Japanese, the two are inextricably merged.

How you dress in Japan says who you are, not as a slogan in the *Esquire* or *GQ* sense, but in the sense that the number of stripes on a uniform represents a rank in the military. For example, Japanese women of a certain age shun certain colors. Until recently, only girls wore red, and certain fabrics were worn exclusively in certain seasons regardless of actual temperature. Thus, a major deviation from standard rules of dress may result in your being mistaken for something that you are not. A bank vice president who uses an obviously cheap pen will simply not register with Japanese counterparts as "bank vice president."

Japanese do not discriminate between form and substance.

The requirements of the Japanese business "dress code" may be summarized as uniformity and quality. Japanese feel quite comfortable and not the least bit constrained by "uniforms." But they insist on quality.

Every Japanese businessperson once wore the school uniforms required throughout elementary and high school. School uniforms are almost universally black, although girls' uniforms may occasionally be deep navy. Differences among uniforms from different schools are virtually undiscernible to an outsider. Many Japanese remember their school uniforms with nostalgia.

Even today, businesspeople simply do not deviate from the dark-suit, white-shirt, plain-black-oxfords model. To the extent that there is even minor deviation, for example, wingtips, or pastel shirts, such deviations are generally the province of people associated with the arts, advertising, marketing, and the like rather than bankers.

Choice is exercised, to some extent, for leisure wear. Nevertheless, Japanese tend to dress more formally than would Americans for a similar occasion and feel most comfortable sporting well-known labels. What Japanese call *rafu*, the equivalent of "casual" derived from the English "rough," may seem a bit stiff by American standards. A Japanese family, especially if new to America, might show up at a backyard barbecue with the father wearing navy blazer and slacks, the mother a dress and high heels, and the children in what looks to Americans like their Sunday best. At a picnic or other casual event including a mixed group of Japanese and Americans, the Americans generally dress in accordance with the host's assurance that blue jeans are appropriate; Japanese adults, however, unless they have lived in the West a long time, will almost never be able to bring themselves actually to wear blue jeans, let alone sweat pants.

Quality is of overriding importance to Japanese both in clothing and accessories. Only a well-known, top-of-the-line pen such as Mont Blanc or Pelikan is acceptable. No businessperson would ever be caught using a 79-cent pen. Nor would any businessperson use a disposable lighter in public. So long as an item of clothing or an accessory can be identified as being of good quality, originality is unimportant. An F.O.B. generally has no particular sense of discomfort or shame about wearing the same $1,500 suit day after day and is unlikely to understand that his doing so may generate negative comment from American colleagues.

Shopping streets in American cities that cater to the carriage trade have come to depend upon Japanese to load up on Dunhills, Burberries, and Chanels. This Japanese penchant to buy expensive name brands reflects more than the current strength of the yen; it coincides perfectly with the need to express the wearer's recognition of quality and, more important, the need to conform to the perceived requirements of a given status.

BOWING

An erroneously simplistic view, often held by both Japanese and Americans, is that bowing in modern Japan is the equivalent of the Western handshake. Out of this mutual misunderstanding, an ad hoc protocol for first meetings between Japanese and Westerners seems to have developed in the last decade: An abbreviated bow is executed concurrently with shaking hands.

At least at home and among themselves abroad, Japanese bow much more often than Westerners shake hands. Japanese who are even slightly acquainted simply cannot pass one another at work, in the neighborhood, or anywhere else for that matter, without performing some type of bow, ranging from a quick nod to a 90-degree bend, depending upon the respective status of the persons bowing. Even coworkers who in the course of an ordinary day pass each other several times are obliged to bow, however slightly.

Obviously, the same circumstances do not call for shaking hands in the West. Often Japanese who are doing business for the first time in the West offer their hands at inappropriate moments because they feel the need to bow and know just enough to know that Westerners shake hands rather than bow.

Over the ages, Japanese have developed an elaborate etiquette of bowing, which they take seriously. Young recruits for sales positions are trained to bow properly. The spine must be held straight with head and shoulders kept on the same plane for the duration of the bow. Eyes must be kept down and feet must be kept together. Men keep their arms at their sides, palms turned in. Women keep their arms down in front of them with palms turned in. The correct number of bows, their angle, and their duration depend principally upon respective rank, but also upon the relative formality or emotional intensity of the occasion. The rules are that the lower ranking bow lower and longer than do the higher ranking, which usually means that younger bow lower and longer than older, and women usually bow lower and longer than men. Occasionally, one person recovers from a bow only to discover that the other person is still down. The first person then feels compelled to go down again. If mutual timing remains out of synch, the result can be an up down-down up performance that Westerners often find comical.

Of course, Japanese do not expect Westerners to be carefully schooled in the art of bowing. Nevertheless, bowing presents a situation where a little knowledge can be dangerous. A typical mistake Americans make is to bow too deeply and too long. A high-level executive of a large corporation who does so makes a mockery of the situation if he bows too obsequiously for his office or for the status of the organization that he represents. On the other hand, a humble bow by a high-ranking person who is making an apology will be greatly admired. In fact, even S.O.B.s are apt to perceive a tincture of insincerity, however unintended, in an apology that is not accompanied by a bow.

The reaction of the Japanese press to an accident, and its aftermath, involving an American submarine and a Japanese merchant vessel illustrates the point. In 1981, an American submarine was on maneuvers in the East China Sea a few hundred miles south of Kyushu. One evening, the submarine scraped the bottom of the Japanese ship, resulting in the loss of two Japanese lives and damage to the Japanese ship. Official Japanese protest regarding the incident was met with a denial by Washington that an American ship had been involved. The denial drew very negative reactions from the Japanese press. Subsequently, the U.S. Navy admitted that the incident had involved one of its submarines; however, the admission included statements that it had been a very dark night and that the incident had not been immediately reported to Navy brass.

Anti-American sentiment in the Japanese media only increased after the Navy's statement. However, a complete reversal occurred after a picture appeared showing Mike Mansfield, then ambassador to Japan, visiting the Japanese foreign ministry in Tokyo, apologizing for the American role in the incident—and bowing deeply. The picture appeared again and again and was met with articles in the Japanese press extolling Ambassador Mansfield as an American who could really understand Japanese sensibilities. Despite the fact that he was not fluent in their language, the Japanese even today regard Mike Mansfield as the most highly respected American ambassador to Japan.

The picture of Ambassador Mansfield bowing and apologizing to the Japanese foreign minister affected Americans and Japanese very differently. Its appearance in *Newsweek* and other publications irritated many Americans who perceived Mansfield's bow as kowtowing to Japanese in much the same way as downed American pilots were forced to kowtow to their North Vietnamese captors during the war in Vietnam.

GESTURES

People who must communicate with each other in the absence of knowledge of one another's language resort to physical gestures, either as a total substitute for words or to buttress meaning when they are only partially capable of communicating verbally. The effort to communicate through gesture is based on the often erroneous assumption that physical gestures are somehow universal, as though they were programmed into human genes.

The assumption may appear to be correct if the gesturing takes place between Westerners. An American who returns from, say, a trip to France or Switzerland may report, "Even though I don't speak a word of French I was able to communicate with the local shopkeepers; it was like playing charades."

Being able to recognize three Japanese gestures that indicate consternation or hesitation is especially important in business negotiations.

Many gestures that share at least approximately common meanings in Western countries do not translate in Asia. In fact, identical gestures may mean something entirely different in Japan that they do in the United States Moreover, the entire status of gestures differs in Japan: Japanese often use gestures when they could perfectly well communicate the same thing verbally. However, gestures are often considered "softer," in the sense of being somehow more subtle or polite. By contrast, Americans consider verbal statements to be more formal and polite than gestures. It would be inappropriate in the United States to signal a high ranking person with a gesture, especially if he is within hearing distance.

The purpose of introducing Japanese gestures is not to encourage Westerners visiting Japan to use them; unless a foreigner is fluent in Japanese, the attempt to use Japanese physical gestures falls flat. We have even seen foreigners who are fluent in Japanese create a sense of caricature by using exclusively Japanese physical gestures. Nevertheless, it is important to know some of the basic ones, first, in order to understand what the Japanese mean and, second, in order to avoid using ones that the Japanese are likely to misinterpret.

Being able to recognize three Japanese gestures that indicate consternation or hesitation is especially important in business negotiations. The first, performed only by males, is scratching the back of the head; the second is inhaling audibly through the teeth; and the third is putting the palm to the forehead. Sometimes a Japanese will perform these gestures *seriatim* in the span of a few seconds. Uninitiated Americans tend either to ignore these gestures and go right on talking or to ask questions such as "What's the matter?" or "Do you have a problem?" The best response, however, is none at all. Simply wait until the gesturing ceases and the Japanese person says something. This waiting period can amount to 10 to

30 excruciatingly long seconds, or even longer. The Japanese will not feel uncomfortable during the silence. To keep the playing field even, Americans should train themselves to be equally at ease watching a succession of "strange" gestures.

Other gestures worth knowing are the following:

1. A thumb pointed in the air means "my boss," *not* as in the United States where the same gestures means "good," "well done," or "go ahead."

2. A circle made with the thumb and index finger means "coin," "money," or "zero," *not* as in the United States where the same gesture means "O.K."

3. Brushing one index finger over the top of the other is meant to look like traditional Japanese sword fighting and indicates that two individuals or groups are at loggerheads, *not* as in the United States where the identical gesture means "shame on you."

4. Circling with the index finger near the ear means "he's crazy" in both countries, but in Japan the gesture is not performed casually—in other words, the person who is being described is thought to be literally insane.

5. An open hand held vertically in front of the chest, usually accompanied by a shallow bow means "excuse me"—the gesture is often used by someone leaving a meeting who is spared by what in the United States would be the expectation that the departure would be explained.

6. The hand held in the same position as in gesture 5 but fanned side to side across the chest means "no thank you," "I don't want any," or "don't do it to me."

7. The right arm outstretched with the hand fanning downward means "please come this way"—Americans sometimes misinterpret the gesture as waving good-bye.

8. Mimicking writing on the palm in a restaurant or bar means that the check is being requested.

9. Mimicking the use of an abacus (*soroban*) means "I [or you] will do the calculation."

10. Two fingers tapped against the palm, which to Japanese eyes mimics the preparation of *sushi*, means "let's knock off work and go to a *sushiya* (sushi bar)."

11. Raising the index finger and pointing to, or actually touching the tip of one's nose means "I am" or "I'll do it."

12. Bringing the palm to the chest means "I have the confidence and I know that I can do it." It is not a gesture that is used often.

Of course, this list is only a brief beginning. You will be able to make your own additions to it after spending some time with the Japanese.

To summarize,

1. Japanese bow more frequently than Americans shake hands.

2. A bow to someone of lower rank should be briefer and shallower than his bow to you.

3. Any serious apology must be unequivocal and be accompanied by a deep bow.

4. Formal and conservative dress is important when meeting Japanese businesspeople.

5. Recognizably high-quality accessories must be part of your wardrobe.

6. When encountering Japanese physical gestures expressing consternation, you must resist the impulse to ask "What's the matter?"

7. Any impulse to use Japanese gestures yourself should be resisted.

8. A familiar gesture used by a Japanese does not necessarily mean the same thing that it means in the United States.

14 Communicating Through Gifts

For Japanese, giving gifts is not an optional nicety or a spontaneous expression of thanks, love, and so on. Rather, it is an institutionalized requirement for establishing and maintaining virtually all types of relationships, including business relationships. Gifts in the Japanese business world are no more dispensable than are business lunches in New York. Japanese businesspeople often maintain a log of gifts they have given and gifts they have received right alongside their rolodexes. Even the value of gifts may be recorded. The importance of gift giving is reflected in the fact that it is responsible for a $92 billion market that is considered to be growing all the time.

Japanese gift-giving practices express basic Japanese cultural traits. *Wa* is promoted by long-term, stable relationships. Gift giving buttresses these relationships. Who gives what to whom and when is rarely a matter of happenstance, but is entirely predictable by reference to long-standing custom. In other words, like so many other factors in Japanese life, gift giving has been refined and ritualized over a long period of time.

It is definitely worthwhile for Americans to learn and practice the rules of the gift-giving game. Too many Americans make the mistake of viewing Japanese gift giving as simply an expensive, time-consuming nuisance rather than as an opportunity to cultivate important business relationships.

Of course, it is hard not to view it as a nuisance when it means packing an extra suitcase with gifts on a trip to Japan. There are practical solutions to the physical problems of delivering large numbers of gifts. One solution is to ship them in advance. Some seasoned American businesspeople manage to acquire wrapping paper from well-known American stores, then purchase American goods after they have arrived in Japan.

Too many Americans make the mistake of viewing Japanese gift giving as simply an expensive, time-consuming nuisance rather than as an opportunity to cultivate important business relationships.

Some Americans believe that they detect an unsavory aspect to what appears to them as otherwise inexplicable extravagance. For example, during the Reagan presidency, two Japanese journalists who had been allowed to interview Nancy Reagan presented her with a pair of gold watches. The gifts received negative attention in the American press as bordering on bribery. However, the Japanese public considered the gold watches a fitting choice for a person of Mrs. Reagan's stature. The watches were not understood as a quid pro quo for granting the interview, but as a token of genuine gratitude that could not be adequately expressed in words. The Japanese never really understood what the fuss over the gold watches was all about.

Japanese rarely overlook opportunities to give gifts. No occasion is considered too meager for gift giving. Japanese give when Americans do: weddings, birthdays,[1] anniversaries, business openings, deal closings, hospitalization, and the like. In addition, there are other times that traditional-minded Japanese consider gift giving an absolute must.

One such time is during *ochugen*, the midsummer season that occurs between July 15 and August 15. The other such time is *oseibo*, or year end. Businesspeople may set aside whole days to deliver gifts personally to important customers or others who have done them favors. The failure to give a required gift at *oseibo* is an inexcusable breach of business etiquette that does not go unnoticed. Foreigners located in Japan, and even those who frequent Japan are expected to adhere to the custom. They will be reminded of it by the throngs of shoppers and ubiquitous references to year-end gift giving. Both *ochugen* and *oseibo* gifts are typically consumable items, such as gourmet food or liquor. *Oseibo* gifts must be distributed no later than December 31.

---

[1]Birthdays are traditionally less important in Japan as gift-giving occasions than they are in the United States.

Gifts given at either of these seasons are given only by subordinates to superiors, from supplier to customer, from department head to division head, and so on. In a country where the "customer is king," these gifts may be viewed as something in the nature of a royal tribute.

Americans should not overlook the opportunity to give a year-end gift, identified as such, to Japanese businesspeople located in the United States. Even the most seasoned S.O.B. will be impressed and gratified by the gesture. The American who gives such a gift, accompanied by the appropriate expression of thanks for past kindnesses, distinguishes his gift from the run-of-the-mill Christmas fruitcake and himself as someone who has taken the time to learn how important the season and its customs are to Japanese.

Japanese merchants have been quick to exploit American holidays for their commercial value as additional opportunities for gift giving, and in recent years, for sending cards. Christmas, Mother's Day, and Father's Day in particular are heavily promoted and advertised in Japan, especially in the major cities. Even Valentine's Day and St. Patrick's Day have infiltrated Japanese commercial culture.

In their haste to exploit American holidays for their commercial value, Japanese do not always manage to keep things quite straight. A journalist for an American newspaper recently reported seeing greeting cards in Japan that combined images of Christmas and Halloween. One such card showed Santa Claus cavorting in a graveyard with scantily clad vampires. The other depicted the Virgin Mary riding on a broomstick.[2]

Apart from designated occasions, it is important to bring gifts to your Japanese hosts. "Hosts" is used here in the broadest possible sense and includes everyone you meet in Japan with whom you have, or wish to establish, a relationship, as well as anyone associated with an organization with which you do or desire to do business. Since it cannot always be anticipated how many people you will be meeting, it is strongly recommended that you bring a surplus of small gifts, wrapped and ready to be distributed as needed.

Gifts given in this context are called *omiyage*, which literally means "souvenir." The name originates in the custom of bringing back gifts whenever a Japanese travels away from home. Goods available exclusively in the locale that the traveler has visited are given as gifts to the traveler's associates who were not on the trip. Japanese business visitors to the United States literally spend whole days and hundreds of dollars buying *omiyage*.

The custom derives from the time, well within the authors' memo-

---

[2]Ronald E. Yates, "An Odd Angle on 'Kurisumasu'" *The Chicago Tribune*, December 23, 1990.

ries, when a wide variety of goods were distributed only locally, and foreign goods were relatively rare. While today practically anything produced either domestically or abroad is widely available in most places in Japan, the custom of giving gifts that are associated with the place where someone has come from persists. Accordingly, a Japanese returning to Tokyo from a business trip to Hiroshima is expected to return with special Hiroshima-style rice cakes, or *sake* produced only in Hiroshima.[3]

Japanese business visitors to the United States literally spend whole days and hundreds of dollars buying *omiyage*.

A good way to show special consideration for a Japanese business visitor is to accompany and assist him on a shopping trip. It is a gesture that will be remembered and appreciated, and you may even succeed in selling *on*.

Omiyage that an American brings to Japan should be as characteristically "American" as possible. This requirement can be filled in several ways. Famous American brand names are much appreciated as are items that incorporate images of well-known American landmarks in the giver's locale if they are of exceptional quality. Good quality items bearing your company's logo are equally prized. Other thoughtful options are leather products or American liquor, both of which are exorbitantly expensive in Japan. Finally, it is not necessary that the gift be for the personal use of the person to whom it is being given. It is quite appropriate to bring a businessman a gift for the use of one of his family members, such as a leather handbag for his wife. A Japanese businessman will also be pleased if you know enough about his family to bring something for his children.

You must also bring a gift on each occasion that you are invited to a Japanese home, no matter how many times you may be invited to the same house. Such gifts are almost always food or beverages.

In selecting gifts, it is important to bow to the Japanese sense of hierarchy. Care must be taken not to offend by giving a significantly higher-ranking person a gift of equal or lesser value than his subordinate. When both giver and recipient are high ranking, say at the vice president

---

[3]Nowadays many Japanese lighten their load by buying "local" products in specialty shops that are located in major train stations and airports for the convenience of the traveler who purchases these products after he returns from a trip. It is a custom that foreigners in Japan also pick up.

level and above, it is not uncommon for them to exchange gifts worth hundreds of dollars. Exceptionally expensive gifts are also in order when a very substantial transaction, such as a joint venture or a long-term contract, is contemplated.

The same care used in selection of a gift must be devoted to wrapping it. Wrapping with American-style wrapping paper or paper embossed with the logo of a well-known American purveyor should be precise and aesthetic. The gift should always be carried and delivered in a bag to demonstrate the giver's modesty. An alternative to a bag is the traditional *furoshiki*, a decorative cloth wrapping that today has in itself become part of the gift. It should be handed to the recipient with both hands and accompanied by a bow and a humble expression of the gift's "worthlessness" regardless how expensive it is. The most typical expression used in presenting a gift is best translated as "this is an unworthy trifle, but please accept it *tsumaranai mono desu, kedo*. Literally, the expression means this is an uninteresting thing, but . . . ." This ritualized humility is meant to express the giver's belief in the importance of the relationship over that of the gift.

Do not be disappointed that despite the time and effort you have devoted to selecting and wrapping a gift, the recipient is apt to refrain from opening it in your presence. Not opening the gift in front of the giver is meant as a consideration for the giver's feelings; just in case the gift is patently *tsumaranai*, the giver's "face" will be saved. In addition, the recipient is spared having to display emotion in response to a truly extravagant gift.

Traditionally, Japanese do not send thank you notes for gifts, although Japanese greeting card manufacturers are increasingly alive to the advantages of promoting this Western custom that fits so well into Japanese tradition. The recipient of a gift in Japan, however, is required to give thanks at the next face-to-face meeting with the giver with an elaborate description of how the gift was put to use and how much it has been enjoyed. Moreover, it is almost inevitable that a gift given to a Japanese is a gift received. The Japanese recipient will look for an early opportunity to return a gift of similar or greater value. The result is sometimes an escalating cycle of gift giving that even Japanese sometimes regard as a nuisance to be tolerated.

Although Japanese gift-giving customs are becoming somewhat less rigid, gift giving is not diminishing in importance in Japanese society. There may be more leeway in terms of when and how gifts should be given, but certainly no movement not to give them at all. Gift giving remains an important nonverbal means of communication, which is not wise to ignore.

To summarize,

1. Despite the inconvenience, you must always bring gifts to people with whom you seek to do or are doing business in Japan.
2. People of significantly different rank in the same organization should not be given the same gift.
3. Americans should select gifts made in the United States.
4. All gifts should be of excellent quality.
5. Gifts must be wrapped carefully.
6. You will probably need more gifts than you think you will.
7. The Japanese posted in your country should be remembered at the Japanese gift-giving seasons.
8. The giving of a gift must be accompanied by an expression of the gift's "worthlessness."
9. No matter how many times you are invited to the same private home, you must bring a gift each time.

15 Communicating Through Eating and Drinking

Social occasions are often the setting for establishing and reinforcing business relationships and for shifting from the *tatemae* to the *honne* channel of communication.

Since long-term relationships are a prerequisite for successfully doing business with the Japanese, it is important that social occasions leave the participants with a sense that things have gone well, that their relationships have begun to develop or have been strengthened, and that there is a basis for continuing them. Of course, eating and drinking are the most emphasized features of social occasions in Japan as elsewhere.

There is no such thing as universal good manners when it comes to eating and drinking. By American or European standards, traditional Japanese table manners seem nonexistent at best. At worst, they appear to fly in the face of every American rule of table etiquette starting with the Japanese custom of sitting on the floor and ending with deliberate soup slurping and unencumbered burping.

American table manners consist of what seems to some Japanese to be an arbitrary series of rules: Don't put your elbows on the table; don't speak with food in your mouth; don't make noise while you eat. As a group, Anglo-Saxons, even compared to continental Europeans, are viewed by the Japanese as being the most slavish in adhering to table manners.

Japanese sometimes claim that the single Japanese rule governing behavior at the table is that whatever comes naturally is not only permissible but is to be encouraged. Thus, if you are eating hot noodles, of course you have to slurp to avoid burning your lips. If you are drinking hot tea,

111

you must sip it audibly in order to cool it sufficiently. If you are drinking beer, you must not suppress a belch. Furthermore, because belching is natural when drinking beer, an apology is uncalled for. If you are eating small pieces of food served in small bowls, *miso* (bean paste) soup, or rice, it is only natural to pick up the bowl, bring it to your face, and shovel mouthfuls of food into your mouth with your chopsticks in order to be efficient and at the same time avoid spills. In fact, not picking up the bowl makes an eater look lazy, unenthusiastic, or lacking in appreciation for the food. Hunching over the plate is also a perfectly acceptable posture that fulfills a similar purpose.

Anyone who has witnessed a formal Japanese tea ceremony where every move is planned and executed with exquisite precision should not be surprised that the truth is that Japanese table manners might be better described as a stylized, even ritualized, form of what is deemed "natural." Therefore, noodles are slurped even if they are not terribly hot. Tea is somewhat audibly sucked through the lips. In a formal tea ceremony, drinking the last drop of tea must be accompanied by a deliberate lip smacking.

In Japan, an employee who fouls up the seating arrangements for an important occasion involving upper level management can actually get demoted.

Knowing that Japanese table manners are a stylized version of what is thought to be natural is not really enough to get by in Japan or in entertaining Japanese in a traditional Japanese restaurant in the United States. There are a few rules that must be observed at the Japanese table.

Seating arrangements both in private homes, restaurants, and even in offices during meetings are very important to Japanese and are treated with close attention. Who sits where is a genuinely sensitive matter even for relatively small gatherings. Japanese guests feel that they have been treated well when the seating arrangements are done properly in accordance with formal rules. While informality and casualness are the concrete expression of hospitality in the United States, Japanese feel that they are being treated hospitably if things are done according to form. It is simply a mistake to tell Japanese guests to "sit wherever you like." In Japan, an employee who fouls up the seating arrangements for an important occasion involving upper-level management can actually get demoted.

To arrange the seating of the Japanese guests correctly, it is necessary to know something about traditional Japanese rooms. The principles that apply there are carried over into Western-style rooms and even office conference rooms.

Every formal traditional Japanese room has a *tokonoma*. A *tokonoma* is a discrete area along one wall of a room that is a designated place of honor. The *tokonoma* can be identified by the artwork that is hung there, traditionally a scroll, or where perhaps a flower arrangement or sculpture is placed. It is considered the best spot in the room. The functional equivalent of the *tokonoma* in an office may simply be the wall on which the most expensive painting hangs or simply the location of the best view if the room is in a glass-walled high rise.

The highest-ranking visitor sits with his back to the *tokonoma* or its functional equivalent. This protocol is counter-intuitive for Americans who generally honor visitors by offering them a seat that allows them to look at the artwork or at the view. The Japanese reasoning is that the most honored guest must be placed against an appropriately grand backdrop. Instead of being invited to see the view, the honored guest is invited to become the view.

Guests must never be seated with their backs to the entrance of the room. This custom may hark back to those times when visiting lords or *samurai* were occasionally dealt with treacherously by their hosts. With the visitors' back to the door, would-be attackers gained the advantage of surprise. Placing a visitor with his back to the entrance is thus seen as making him feel vulnerable instead of secure.

In the traditional Japanese seating arrangement, the highest-ranking guest is placed with his back to the center of the *tokonama*. Lower-ranking guests are positioned on either side of him in order of descending rank. The host group is seated on the guest group's left flank with the highest ranking member of the host group closest to the guest group. The lower ranking guests sit along the right flank of the higher-ranking guests, that is, facing the hosts. The traditional arrangement described may be modified in international meetings and sometimes must be modified to accommodate positioning of interpreters.

Japanese social occasions will almost invariably include alcoholic beverages and appetizers in lavish quantities, and may be followed by an equally generous full-course meal. Predinner drinking traditionally takes place while seated as opposed to the vertical American cocktail hour before going in to dinner. Traditional Japanese drinks include *sake* and beer. Western whiskeys have gained popularity since the World War II, and lately *shochu*[1] has been added to the list of favored drinks. Moderate intoxication is quite acceptable in men, and occasional, outright drunkenness is tolerated.

At congratulatory occasions, drinking is often opened with a toast to which the guests may respond by standing, throwing arms in the air, and declaring *banzai!* three times.[2] More informal toasting is accomplished by raising glasses and saying *kampai*, which is the equivalent of "bottoms up."

A drinking custom followed strictly in Japan as well as in most other countries in Asia is that you *never* pour into your own glass. Unless a waiter or waitress is doing the pouring, you must always be attentive to your tablemate's glass. When it reaches the state of being one-third empty, you must fill it again. Your picking up the bottle to perform this function will signal your tablemate to lift his glass or *sake* cup for it to be filled. Your tablemate will fill your glass in the same way. The custom applies to everyone at the table, whether guest or host. Even S.O.B.s who are used to the American custom of filling their own glass will appreciate your knowledge and practice of the Japanese custom if you are comfortable with it.

If you do not wish to drink any more, simply leaving your glass full is quite appropriate. At the end of a drinking session, many glasses are left on the table full or nearly full.

If you cannot or do not wish to drink at all, the way to signal others is to turn your glass or *sake* cup upside down before anything is poured. Anyone who is designated to drive in Japan will not touch a drop of alcohol. The legal penalties for drunk driving in Japan are draconian by American standards. The social penalties for injuring someone on account of driving drunk may be even worse.

Traditional Japanese meals always start with cleaning hands with a hot towel served by the waitress. White rice is always included. The serving of rice sometimes signals the shift from predinner eating and drinking to the main meal. True to Japanese tenets of male chauvinism, the highest-ranking male is served first, followed by the rest of the males in order of rank, then the females, if any are present. If you are entertaining an F.O.B. in the United States, be advised that he may be rankled if a female, especially a younger female, gets her order taken or is served first.

---

[1]*Shochu* is a strong alcoholic beverage made from fermented sweet potatoes. It used to be considered something of a peasant's drink, but has become fashionable among yuppies and students.

[2]*Banzai*, literally means ten thousand years. It has no militaristic overtones in the context of a formal toast.

It may be worthwhile deferring to such a person and alerting others in your organization to do the same.

When you are taking an F.O.B. to a restaurant, be prepared to offer a clear recommendation as to what to order. If a high-ranking F.O.B. is part of a larger group, don't be surprised if the rest of the group orders exactly the same thing as the ranking member.

Following the leader is a gesture of respect. The following anecdote was related by a Japanese American tour guide who was escorting a group of Japanese who were attending an electronic equipment show in Chicago. It was the first trip to the West for most of the members of the group. The group expressed its desire to experience a typical American breakfast. The tour guide took them to one of Chicago's poshest eateries. All the group members diligently studied the menu. The ranking member of the group ordered ham and eggs over easy. The rest of the group members, one by one, ordered the same thing. When the food was delivered, the ranking member, in accordance with impeccable Japanese manners picked up the plate and slurped down the eggs. Virtually in unison, the rest of the group members followed his lead and did exactly the same thing.[3]

No one at a traditional Japanese meal begins eating before the ranking person says *itadakimasu,* which literally means "I will partake of this." The phrase expresses the sentiment of thanks to all who participated in creating the meal. Each person says *itadakimasu* before he or she starts eating, although no one need wait in turn to say it. The meal is officially ended with each person's saying *gochiso-sama deshita,* which means "this was a great feast." The habit of uttering these phrases at the beginning and end of meals is so ingrained that it is not unusual to hear older Japanese saying them out loud even when they are eating alone in a fast-food restaurant.

The implement used to eat Japanese food is Japanese chopsticks.[4] Your Japanese host may excuse you from using chopsticks on your very first trip to Japan, but after that, it will be expected that you use chopsticks without comment. Asians view chopsticks as having no less universality than forks, knives, and spoons.

At a formal meal, chopsticks are placed on a *hashi-makura,* a small

---

[3]Purposeless originality of any kind in the presence of a high-ranking person shows a lack of appropriate deference and may be viewed with disfavor. Japanese have an expression that embodies this norm: *deru kugi wa utareru,* "the nail that sticks out gets hammered down."

[4]Japanese chopsticks are different from Korean and Chinese chopsticks. Japanese chopsticks are pointed and made of wood that is lacquered unless the chopsticks are of the disposable variety. Korean chopsticks are pointed and are usually made of silver. Many Korean dishes are eaten with chopsticks and a large spoon. Chinese chopsticks have blunt ends and are rarely lacquered.

decorative ceramic slab, parallel to the edge of the table. When not in use, chopsticks should be returned to the *hashi-makura* or placed parallel to one another on a low-lying plate. They should never be parked vertically in a rice bowl. While untutored foreigners may find it convenient to do so, to Japanese eyes it looks ridiculously childish, like an adult holding a spoon in a clenched fist.

Sometimes food is place on a communal serving plate. Unless there are additional chopsticks designated for serving, you may use your own chopsticks to transfer food to your own plate. However, you must flip them around, pick up the food with the clean end, transport the morsel of food onto one of your plates, and flip the chopsticks back to the business end to put the food into your mouth.

A final note on chopsticks: Food is never passed from one person's chopsticks to another's. The reason is that at Japanese funerals it is customary for relatives to transfer the burnt bones of the deceased from one person to another with chopsticks. A meal is not the time to evoke the imagery of cremation.

When the meal is over, who pays? First, bills are never split in Japan regardless of amount. Paying is a ministerial task to be accomplished with utmost subtlety and is left to a lower-ranking person. Often arrangements for payment have been made in advance of the occasion. In many cases, the host organization has an account at the restaurant or bar, and nothing at all is said or done regarding payment in the presence of guests. The American way of paying, where the senior person studies the bill to determine its correctness, then takes out his credit card in full view of the guests, is considered uncouth by Japanese standards. If you want an F.O.B. to feel completely comfortable, it is best for the group to get up and prepare to leave while a junior colleague is left slightly behind to pay.

To summarize,

1. When you are hosting a Japanese, especially an F.O.B.,
   - Be attentive to seating arrangements.
   - Be prepared to recommend what to order.
   - Be sure that the ranking F.O.B. is served first.
   - Be subtle at payment time.

2. In Japan
   - Never pour an alcoholic beverage into your own glass.
   - Keep you tablemate's glass filled.
   - Never offer to split the bill.
   - Learn to use chopsticks.
   - Remember to say *itadakimasu* and *gochiso-sama deshita*.

Conclusion

Deals should fall apart when there are substantive reasons for not doing them. They should not fall apart because the potential dealmakers don't know whom they are talking to or have nary a clue as to what the person they are talking to is really saying and thinking. Neither American nor Japanese businesspeople can afford ignorance as to who the other is.

The thoroughgoing internationalization of markets has taken place with astonishing rapidity and continues apace. Still, many American managers and entrepreneurs have had relatively little international experience. Their formal education, in all likelihood, was not geared toward cross-cultural encounters. The experience and wisdom of their seniors, who could build whole careers in the territory between Chicago and Peoria, may not be of much help when it comes to doing business between Peoria and Osaka.

For Americans, many Japanese ways of communication are counter-intuitive, awkward, or simply opaque, just as American ways can seem startling and abrasive in Japanese eyes. It is hoped that this book has helped you to prepare for understanding and working with the Japanese by enabling you to avoid misinterpreting the Japanese and to understand how the Japanese may be interpreting you. Application of the knowledge that you have acquired—for example, that silence on the part of a Japanese is not necessarily rejection, that talking about family and hobbies at business meetings with Japanese is not a side track, that a sincere apology gets you farther with the Japanese than an unfullfilled promise—will go a long way in making you more effective with the Japanese.

Of course, reading this book is not the same as being touched by a magic wand; it cannot transmogrify an American reader into a skilled practitioner of *haragei* any more than reading a book could turn a Japanese businessperson into a gregarious egalitarian. However, you are now much better poised to take full advantage of additional lessons offered by future experience.

Guide to Pronouncing Japanese Words

For native speakers of English, pronunciation of Japanese words poses very few difficulties. The number of sounds used in Japanese is far fewer than the number in English. Furthermore, 99 percent of the sounds used in Japanese exist in English. As a result, it is much easier for English speakers to pronounce Japanese words than for Japanese speakers to pronounce English words. Of the few problems English speakers do typically experience, most are on account of the necessity of transcribing the thousands of Japanese characters and phonetic symbols into the Roman alphabet.

VOWELS

There are only five vowel sounds in Japanese as compared to sixteen or seventeen in English. These five vowel sounds are represented as "a," "i," "u," "e," "o" and pronounced as follows:

"A" is pronounced as the "a" in father, never as the "a" in "cat."

"I" is pronounced as the "e" in eat, never as the "i" in light.

"U" is pronounced as the "oo" in book, never as the "u" in "cute."

"E" is pronounced as the "e" in "let."

"O" is pronounced as what might be described as a shortened version of the "o" in "horn." There is no precise English equivalent. "O" is never pronounced as the "o" in "hot."

Sometimes "i" and "u" are virtually skipped when they appear between two consonants. "U" is also sometimes skipped at the end of a word. For example, the word "sukoshi," meaning "a little" is pronounced as though it were written as "s'koshi." The name of the corporate giant, "Matsushita," is pronounced as though it were written "Matsush'ta." The "disappearance" of these vowels is similar to what happens to "i" in the word "business." The very common word "desu," meaning "is" or "are" is pronounced as though it were written "des."

Japanese distinguish short from long vowel sounds. Sometimes this distinction is made clear in the romanized spelling of a word. For example, "obasan" means "aunt" while "obaasan," in which the "a" sound is drawn out, means "mother."

Unfortunately, the typical romanization of some Japanese words does not preserve the distinction between long and short vowels. For example, to reflect the correct pronunciation, the capital city of Japan should probably be romanized as "To'okyo'o" or "Tohkyoh" rather than its almost universal rendition as "Tokyo."

CONSONANTS

Most Japanese consonants have a virtually identical counterpart in English. Again, however, certain pronunciation problems attributable to the necessity of romanization may occur. For example, when two consonants appear together, such as in the word "Hokkaido" (the northernmost major island in the Japanese archipelago), there is a short, but discernible, hesitation between the two "k"s.

There is a series of sounds in Japanese, romanized as the letter "r," that is quite different from the "r" sound in American English. The Japanese sounds represented by "r" are very slightly trilled and sound something like a combination of "d" and "l." Picking up this sound takes a sharp ear and a little practice.

ACCENT

English speakers accentuate one or more syllables in multisyllabic words by stressing them. For example, the syllabication and pronunciation of the word "punctuality" is shown in the dictionary as "punk′ cho͞o,-al′ə-ti," indicating a primary stress on the third syllable and a secondary stress on the first syllable.

To the extent that Japanese speakers accentuate syllables within words at all, they do so by a change in pitch. For example, the difference between "hashi" meaning "bridge" and "hashi" meaning "chopsticks" depends upon which syllable is given the higher pitch: "Ha| s̄h̄i" with a rising pitch is "bridge," while "h̄ā|s̲h̲i̲" with a falling pitch is "chopsticks."

The only way to learn the pitch patterns of particular Japanese words is to hear them. However, pitch in Japanese is incomparably simpler than in Chinese where there can be as many nine distinct patterns of pitch, depending upon dialect. By contrast, pitch errors by foreign speakers of Japanese only rarely cause misunderstandings.

Glossary of Japanese Terms

Amae: A term to describe the uniquely Japanese form of the psychology of interdependence between two persons. The prototypical form of *amae* is embodied in the relationship between an infant and its mother. *Amaeru* is a verb form of the same word, meaning "to be sweet to another."

Banzai: A formal toast which literally means "ten-thousand years."

Bengoshi: A lawyer. To become a *bengoshi,* a person must pass an extraordinarily difficult bar examination. Very few take the exam and still fewer pass it.

Bucho: Literally, "division head." However, people of comparable rank in American business organizations are usually designated as vice-presidents.

Chan: Form of address used for young children or children of any age within the family.

Dohai: See *sempai.*

Enryo: See *omoiyari.*

Fukushacho: Literally, "vice-president." The equivalent rank in an American business organization is the person who is literally second in command, such as an executive vice-president or a chief operating officer.

Furoshiki: A decorative square cloth often used to wrap gifts.

Giri: Along with *on,* it is one of the two types of social or personal obligations that Japanese acquire. *Giri* accrues simply by virtue of a person's position within a group.

Gochisosama; gochisosama deshita: An expression of thanks and satisfaction at the conclusion of a meal.

Hai: Literally meaning "yes," its use does not always connote agreement, but may be no more than an indication that a listener is being attentive.

Hancho: Literally, "squad leader." Unlike the corrupted use of the term in English as connoting a powerful person, the term used in Japanese connotes a functionary capable of carrying out someone else's policy.

Hanko: An official seal which serves as the functional equivalent of a signature.

Haragei: Literally meaning "belly art," like "*ishin-denshin*" *haragei* refers to indirect communication and suggestion.

Hirohito: The name of the Japanese emperor who reigned from 1925 to 1989.

Honne: Contrasted to *tatemae,* it literally means "true voice." It is unvarnished truth communicated unofficially between persons who know each other well.

Ishin-denshin: Literally meaning, "if it is in one heart, it will be transmitted to another heart," a common Japanese expression referring to communication without words.

Itadakimasu: An expression of thanks which must be stated before beginning to eat.

Jukunen: A recently coined word meaning "seasoned or ripened age," replacing a traditional word "*ronen*" meaning "old age."

Kacho: Literally, "section chief," the rank denotes someone who has reached middle management.

Kamikaze: Literally, "devine wind." During World War II, the Japanese used the term for the pilots and the airplanes they flew on suicide missions against the U.S. Pacific fleet.

Kampai: Japanese toast meaning "bottoms up."

Kao: Face. It embodies both one's personality and sense of self-worth.

Katakana: One of the two systems of phonetic symbols in Japanese, *katakana* is used exclusively for words of foreign origin. The other system of phonetic symbols is called *hiragana.*

Kohai: See *sempai.*

Koto: A traditional, stringed instrument.

Kun: A term of address used only within an organization for male colleagues of equal or junior rank. It is added as a suffix to the person's name.

Mado no hito: Literally meaning "window people," this term applies to personnel deemed not to be productive. Such people are seated near the window and given little to do. They may spend much of their time looking out of the window.

Mannen-kacho: Literally meaning "ten-thousand year section chief," the term refers to a person who is not destined to advance beyond middle management.

Marugakae: To hire the whole person or an organization, "lock, stock, and barrel."

Meishi: Business cards.

Nemawashi: This term, whose literal meaning is "turning the roots," derives from the horticultural practice of turning roots of a newly planted tree to determine which way it will settle best in the soil. The term is applied in business to the informal communication among the people involved in a particular program, project or decision.

Nihon: Nihon and Nippon, both meaning Japan, are alternate ways of pronouncing the same two-character word.

NHK: Nihon Hoso Kyokai, the Japan Broadcasting Corporation, is a national network of radio and television much like the BBC in Britain.

Nikkei 225: Nikkei is the abbreviation for *Nihon Keizai Shimbun,* the largest financial newspaper in Japan whose Databank Bureau compiles a stock index. *Nikkei* 225 is the benchmark stock index, much like Standard & Poor's 500 in the U.S.

Nikkori: An adverb meaning "with a smile."

Obeyashugi: Literally, meaning "big roomism," the term refers to the typical arrangement in Japanese corporate offices in which dozens of people, including managers, work in the same room.

Ochugen: Midsummer season during which gifts are given from subordinates to superiors.

Okyaku: Literally meaning "honorable guest," the term is used to refer to customers, clients, passengers and the like.

Omiyage: Literally meaning "honorable local product," the giving of *omiyage* by someone who has been away is *de riguer.*

Omoiyari: *Omoiyari* means "showing consideration," and *enryo* means "holding back" when consideration is shown. *Enryo* generally occurs in the *tatemae* mode of communication. A Japanese may extend you an invitation out of a sense of *omoiyari,* but you may decline it at first out of a sense of *enryo.*

On: Along with *giri, on* is one of the two types of social obligation or debt that Japanese incur. *On* arises when someone renders benevolence, mercy or favor going beyond the call of duty. It is said that *on* can never be fully repaid.

Oseibo: Year end season at which gifts are given by subordinates to their superiors.

Ringisno: A document which officially memorializes a plan or strategy after the conclusion of *nemawashi,* or informal discussion.

Ronen: A traditional term for "old age." See *jukunen* above.

Sama: An extremely respectful form of address typically reserved for clients or customers and used as a suffix to the person's family name.

San: The most common form of address used as a suffix to a person's name.

Sempai: Along with *kohai* and *dohai,* the term is one of the three words referring to the relative rank of people who work for the same organization. *Sempai* refers to any senior colleague who entered the organization before you. *Dohai* refers to those who entered the organization at the same time as you. *Kohai* refers to those who entered after you.

Sensei: Used as an independent noun, it means "teacher" or "master." It is also used as a term of address to teachers, lawyers, doctors and to other people who have reached a high level of achievement in the professions or arts.

Shimaguni konjo: Literally, "island nation mentality." An expression often used by Japanese to refer to the negative aspects of their ethnocentricity.

Shinjinrui: Literally "new human species." The term is used somewhat derisively to refer to the new generation of Japanese who were born in the economic affluence of the 1960s and later.

Shochu: An alcoholic beverage made of fermented sweet potatoes.

Shokainin; shokaisha: A "go between" or introducer who vouches for the integrity of the person being introduced.

Shukko: A person "on loan" from another company or from a government agency.

Sogo shosha: A general trading company.

Sumo: Traditional Japanese wrestling.

Soroban: Japanese abacus still in common use in stores and offices.

Tatemae: Literally meaning "facade," the term refers to formal or official channels of communication as contrasted to *honne*.

Tokonoma: A designated place of honor along one wall of a room.

Teishisei: "Low posture style," the term refers to the humble demeanor used to show politeness. It is considered a sign of maturity.

Wa: "Harmony." Many Japanese believe that *wa* is one of the most important sources of any organization's productivity.

Yakuza: Persons involved in Japanese organized crime.

Yamato: An alternate, historical way of referring to Japan. The reference functions much like calling Thailand "Siam," or China "Cathay."

Index

A

Abbreviated bow, 99
Accessories, quality of, 98, 103
Adages, translation of, 85-86
Ageism, 37-39
Agenda, business meetings, 60-61
Alletzhauer, Albert J., 56
Amae, 21-22
Amaterasu, 10
Ambiguity, 17-19
Americans, monochronic perception of time, 29-31
Apology, 78
    and bowing, 100
Are, 18

B

Backslapping, 92
"Belly communication/belly language," *See Haragei*
Bengoshi, 57
Bhuddism, 11-12
Bi-lateral relationships, importance of, iii-iv
Bilingual business cards, 65-66
Blame fixing, Japanese system of, 51
Bowing, 5, 7, 20, 60, 99-100, 103
    abbreviated bow, 99
    American mistakes in performing, 99-100
    and apology, 100
    compared to handshaking, 99
    etiquette of, 99
    and gift giving, 108-9
    and *meishi*, 64
Business cards, 60, 63-67
    American view of, 63

    bilingual, 65-66
    and bowing, 64
    Japanese view of, 63-64
    size/information contained on, 63
    See also Meishi
Business meetings:
    agenda, 60-61
    first meeting, 59-60
Business organizations, 47-53
    horizontal structure, 47-48, 50
    informal communication within, 51
    promotions, 49
    salary, 49-50
    vertical structure, 42, 47-51, 53
    See also Japanese companies

C

Casual attire, 98
-chan, 73
Charisma, of corporate leaders, 52-53
Chigaimasu, 79
Children:
    and emotions, 27
    form of address, 73
China, regional identities, 11
Chopsticks, 115-16
Citizenship, obtaining in Japan, 10
Cohen, Herb, 31
Cold calls, 55-56
Collective good, responding to, 15
Collective identity, 19-20
    amae, 21-22
    enryo, 26-27
    giri, 24-26
    kao, 21